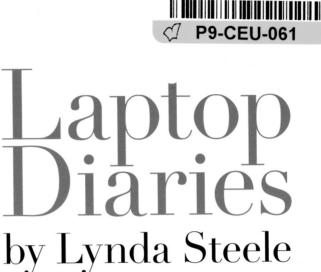

Laptop Diaries

by Lynda Steele

Laura —
Thanks for
your support!

Lynda

Laptop Diaries

by Lynda Steele

Printed in Canada

Library and Archives Canada Cataloguing in Publication

Steele, Lynda, 1960-
    Laptop Diaries / Lynda Steele.

ISBN 978-0-9784531-0-7

    1. Steele, Lynda, 1960- I. Title.

AC8.S68 2007   C818'.603   C2007-905465-X

Printed & Published by McCallum Printing Group Inc.

Acknowledgements:

To my husband and best friend Norm

Mom and Dad, the GNO ladies: Sue, Mo, Kathy D., Kathy T., Gord, Ross, Lisa and Jeff, thanks for your wisdom, friendship and support.

My appreciation to photographer Brenda Bastell for the wonderful cover photography.
(Hair by Jonn Gluwchynski, makeup by Pamela Parker)

Thanks to Tim Spelliscy, Global Edmonton, Allan Mayer and Kathy Kerr, The Edmonton Journal for your guidance.

My appreciation to Chapters, Audrey's Books and Volume II Books which have all generously waived their distribution fees for the cause.

Special thanks to Richard McCallum, McCallum Printing for your generosity and good will – and Rob Prins for your hard work and good humour.

And a final salute to all the hard-working, underpaid shelter workers in Alberta. Thank you for saving literally thousands of lives every year.

Table of Contents

Girl Talk

1

Lynda's GNO Posse… left to right Kathy D., Kathy T., Lynda, Mo, Sue

The GNO

It's hard for guys to truly understand how good female friends can spend 72 hours together, and not run out of things to say.

My husband is always intensely curious to know the topics of conversation at my annual girls' weekend. Did we talk about him? What did everyone say?

How's life going for the ladies? What on earth did we DO for three straight days anyway?

My girls' getaway is dubbed the GNO, that's short for Girl's Night Out.

For the past 11 years, four of my best girlfriends have rearranged life to soak up several days of rest, relaxation and the restorative power of women.

We talk about world conflict, kids, hairstyles, PMS, and career plans. We brainstorm problems, share ideas, and shed a few tears. But mostly we laugh. And eat cheese.

This year's GNO was spent at a rented "villa" in Kelowna that we sussed out on the Internet.

1

Five bedrooms, three bathrooms, a kitchen, and best yet — a full-size outdoor swimming pool surrounded by an acre of flowers and fruit trees.

We settle in poolside, and the three-day conversation begins.

"Why do so many men in their 50s hook up with women half their age?"

"Yeah — I don't know who's more pathetic. The middle-aged guy with a girl who looks like his daughter — or the boobalooba looking for a meal ticket."

"I bet Viagra is directly responsible for the increase in older men pursuing younger women.

"Someone should really do a study."

"Hey are you going inside? Can you bring me a bottle of water from the fridge?"

Yup, it's gonna be another good one. Five friends basking in the hot Kelowna sun, and the warmth of women who love you unconditionally.

It's an idyllic summer setting, and we're utterly charmed when three brown ducklings hop into the pool and begin paddling about.

"Awww, that's so sweet... Look here comes the momma duck!"

It's a saccharine scene until the big bird blows a load of liquid feces into the pool.

"Ewwww...that's so disgusting! Get out of there you little buggers."

The conversation is interrupted temporarily as we run poolside, slapping neon foam noodles into the water to flush the ducks out.

"God that's gross."

"Well what do you think is on the bottom of a lake?"

"Yeah, well I just wish I didn't have to see it, you know?"

The rest of the afternoon is punctuated by laughter and the slamming of the back screen door.

It's a hot, lazy day and the conversation shifts from idle gossip, "Hey you won't believe who just got breast implants!" to world affairs, "OK, call me stupid, but what's the difference between Hezbollah and Hamas?"

We compare bathing suits, and fret about our figures, clucking and comforting...

"What do you mean you look fat? You look fantastic — seriously!"

"No, look at my gut... right around the middle, no matter what I do, it's getting thicker."

"That's called perimenopause sister, get used to it."

And so it goes. Each day slipping into the next. No stress, no worries.

I'm dying for a mid-afternoon nap, but these moments are so precious, I can't bear the thought of missing anything. I don't want to be out of the conversational loop for even 15 minutes. So when the mosquitoes chase us inside, I lie on the couch with eyes closed, one foot in dreamland, one ear still open to the ladies soothing murmur.

"My eyes are closed but I'm still listening... you're having heart problems? What's that all about?"

And then it's over. Incredibly 72 hours has passed, and we're loading the dishwasher, packing our bags and pouring one last cup of coffee for the road.

Five women, five cities, five lives entwined and enriched by the power of female friendships.

One by one we reluctantly depart, lamenting the end of yet another girl's weekend.

At the airport, there's time for one last squishy, extended hug.

"I'm feeling sick to my stomach because I can't believe the weekend is over, and I miss you already."

I love you, too, ladies. Looking forward to the 12th annual GNO. ◼

1

My Not So Secret Purse Fetish

Lord, help me — I've developed a purse fetish, and I blame it all on a puppet.

For years, I worried I was missing a chromosome unique to women that makes them unable to resist cute handbags.

While my girlfriends were sporting the latest hot pink summer hobo bag, I was happily making do with a utilitarian basic black affair. Goes with everything, big enough for all my stuff, trendy, but not too out there, if you know what I mean.

"You can't have a BLACK purse in summertime," my girlfriends would lament.

"Live a little! Buy something fun and kicky. It doesn't have to match your shoes, you know."

It doesn't?

OK, then. I traded in my black leather Nine West handbag for a lime green satin Chinese print purse, and my life has never been quite the same.

1

"Oh, my God - that purse is to DIE for! Where did you get it? Does it come in any other colours?"

Every woman I came in contact with drooled over my funky new handbag.

I felt... hip. I felt... powerful. I felt the pull of a looming addiction.

Even men were entranced.

Alberta's own marionette master, Ronnie Burkett, begged me to hand over the bag.

I was trying to negotiate an interview with the puppeteer for a TV show I was working on. He wanted me to trade the purse for a few hours of his time.

Burkett was premiering a new puppet play, and there was a scene in which a marionette was removed from a case and introduced into the dialogue. He thought my Chinese print bag would make a better prop.

I wanted the interview badly, but I was in love with my little green power purse. And the fact that another person — a man, no less — wanted to take it on an international tour, made it even more precious.

I said no. He said no. And we never spoke again.

Who knew the power of a simple purse? I was hooked.

A red leather handbag caught my eye next. Red! Now that's kicky. I'll take it.

Then I bought a purple leather number, followed by a paisley-print fabric hobo bag, then a brown purse to go with my new brown fall suit. And on it went.

But perhaps my greatest coup was my biggest bargain.

I was strolling down Broadway with my mum during a Mother's Day getaway in New York this spring, when a street vendor's cart caught my eye. Ummm, that's a cute handbag. White's hot this year, isn't it? How much?

"That bag is $30." The street vendor looked a bit bored.

My mum was bored too, anxious to get back to the hotel to put up her feet.

"Oh, just leave it," she sighed. "You can get one tomorrow; those kiosks are everywhere."

That got the vendor's attention. Sensing he was about to lose a sale, he blurted out: "OK. For you, a special deal today — $25!"

I hesitated. It really was pretty cute, and a good size too, with all these funky little zippers and tassels everywhere. By now, Mom was literally grabbing my elbow.

"Come on," she implored. "Let's go have a coffee somewhere, you can get it later."

"Twenty dollars!" the vendor beseeches.

Twenty dollars? I'm pulling out my wallet now. That's a great little handbag for 20 bucks.

When I got back to Edmonton, my new white purse from New York got plenty of attention from local fashionistas.

"Is that a Balenciaga?" one woman purred. "The designer motorcycle bag from the 1990s?"

A Balenciaga-who? "Uh, I paid $20 at a street vendor's cart in New York."

Apparently I bought a knock-off designer bag, and a good one at that.

It was the best $20 I ever spent.

My white motorcycle bag was functional and funky, and it trumped my green satin Chinese purse by a royal flush or two.

If I had a toonie for every compliment I got on that discount handbag, I could practically fly back to New York and buy another one.

Alas, all good things must come to an end. After a summer of dragging my fake Balenciaga bag around town, it's got pen marks on the exterior, and grime on the bottom and handles that won't rub off.

So I've reluctantly made a decision. I'm keeping my beloved bag until the end of September, and then it's going to Goodwill.

I confess to being a bit sad, actually. But hey, have you seen the fabulous handbags out this fall? ■

1

(left to right J'lyn, Lynda & professional bra fitter Dawn Bell

Make Mine A Double…D

Knockers, hooters, jugs, ta ta's, melons, bazookas, bazongas, headlights, rack, the twins, the girls, or just plain old boobs.

They come in all shapes and sizes, both god given and man made.

We love them - we hate them. We wish they were bigger, smaller, perkier.

We spend millions of dollars on wisps of lace and moulded underwire to prop them up, and show them off, yet experts say 80 per cent of women have no idea what their actual bra size is.

Come on admit it. The bra you're wearing right now - is it really comfortable? Do you have rolls of back fat showing through your sweater? Are the straps falling off your shoulders?

How many bras have you bought in your lifetime that looked great on the store mannequin with it's perfectly plastic breasts, but ended up in your bottom drawer because it was too uncomfortable to wear for more than a couple of hours?

Well sister, I feel your pain, and I'm here to tell you that all it takes is one hour

---

of your time to eliminate a lifetime of discomfort.

"I have lots of women cry in the fitting room."

Dawn Bell knows bras. She grew up in her grandmother's Regina bra shop and learned how to fit brassieres from a master. She now owns her own store in Edmonton called Dawn's Bratique, and her mission is to end the suffering caused by ill fitting bras that look bad and make women feel worse.

"I've had older ladies walk into the fitting room with a cane, and once they put on the right size bra… walk right out and forget their cane."

Bell says a bad bra can cause everything from posture problems to migraines. Women just get used to the discomfort and live with it.

Was I one of those women? There was only one way to find out. I gathered a small posse of girlfriends, and fortified by a glass of wine over lunch, we made our way to Dawn's Bratique for a professional fitting.

We were a little nervous. Would we have to stand naked in front of a stranger? Thankfully no. Everyone got their own fitting room, and a "starter" bra in the size we were currently wearing.

"I look like something from the Jetson's – they're pointy!" J'lyn shrieked with laughter from the fitting room next door.

Dawn moved from stall to stall giving each of us a professional assessment, and then handed us bras in the size we "should" be wearing.

"Are you supposed to lean over and hike them up?" My friend Kim whispered through the dressing room wall.

It's amazing what a properly fitting bra can do for both your physique and your mood. You actually look slimmer, and feel more comfortable when the shoulder and back straps sit where they're supposed to.

Turns out all three of us were wearing the wrong bra size. We were all actually one cup size bigger. I guess it's not surprising when you consider your bra size changes about six times in your life, yet most middle-aged women are still wearing the same size bra they did in high school.

"They don't want to be a G cup," Dawn explains, "but wearing a D cup is not going to help, it's going to make you uncomfortable and grumpy."

Some women are so hung up on size, they refuse to buy a pair of panties if the tag says large. The seamstress at Dawn's Bra-tique has actually sewn fake labels into lingerie to make customers feel better about themselves.

But really, who cares what the tag says? I say if the bra fits...

"Oh my breasts look spectacular!"

And with that delighted comment, our bra fitting adventure was over. J'lyn was so tickled, she decided to leave her utility Wonderbra in the fitting room and wear her new model home. At the till we got more good news - it turns out the store donates clean, used bras to the WIN House women's shelter.

So ladies - do yourself a favour. Don't spend one more week wearing the wrong bra size.

Go for a professional fitting. I guarantee "the girls" will thank you for it. ■

1

The Great Nylons Conspiracy

I hate nylons.

My last pair cost $15. High-end hose for an office cocktail party. They lasted exactly five minutes. I took off my coat, walked ten steps, and felt my toe punch through. The rest of the night was spent looking for nail polish, and obsessing over the run slowly creeping up my right foot.

I'm no math whiz, but I figure those nylons cost me about $3 a minute.

It's a corporate conspiracy. A sick joke perpetrated on women, designed to either make us broke or drive us batty.

And you can blame it all on a man. An American chemist named Wallace Carothers.

In 1935 he invented nylon for the DuPont company. It was originally called "no-run" later modified to "nylon", and was patented as "a see-through, glossy fibre which is tear-proof, shock-resistant, heat-resistant and indestructible."

Yeah, tell it to my friend Sandra. She's a TV news anchor in Ottawa, who was minutes away from emceeing the biggest event of the year, The Snowflake Ball, when disaster struck.

"While I was being introduced, I did my best to strike a pose at the table… smiled winningly, crossed one knee over the other — hit the bottom of the table with my knee and promptly ripped a huge hole smack dab on the kneecap. 'Ladies and Gentlemen, please help me welcome Sandra Blaikie!' Oh my god."

It's hard to believe that women used to engage in fist fights for the right to purchase and wear this annoying product.

In the mid-1940s, nylons were in huge demand, and ladies desperate to get their hands on a pair of hose actually caused riots outside American department stores.

What were they thinking?

1

These days, women might riot just to force manufacturers to put out a product that actually lasts more than two wearings, and doesn't cost a fortune.

Not to mention they're uncomfortable — too hot, too short, too tight, saggy crotch, baggy ankles, circulation-cutting waistbands.

I was thrilled when spray-on nylons hit the drugstore, until I spent five minutes applying the product, and 15 minutes trying to clean the greasy, brown mess out of my bathtub.

My friend Sue has sworn off hose, but as a tango dancer, occasionally needs to wear nylons for a gala event.

She tried pull-ups to avoid overheating "only to have the elastic in the right leg explode after one dance, leaving a nylon clump around my carefully extended ankle. Oh so elegant."

Oh so aggravating.

Some women are saying to hell with it, and going bare-legged to the office. What would the fashionistas say?

"I hate nylons."

Rita Silvan is editor-in-chief of Elle Canada magazine. "I find them itchy, and my body feels like it's encased in sausage wrapping."

Rita hasn't worn nylons in 18 years, and says pantyhose are passe. Her advice? If your work environment is casual, go without.

If not… "Then choose the right pantyhose for your skin tone… the right texture so they're not too heavy. And don't use them as a camouflage technique. If you need to shave your legs, then do!"

And if you want some tips on making your nylons last, try these four star ideas culled from Internet chat sites.

1. Wash new nylons before you wear them. It loosens fibres, making them less likely to run.

2. Washing then freezing new nylons will make them last even longer.

3. Spraying nylons lightly with hairspray before wearing helps prevent snags and runs.

4. Wear gloves while putting on your hose to avoid ripping them.

And if that doesn't work, say a little prayer for the golden orb-weaving spider. The strength of its dragline silk has amazed scientists with its ability to stretch without snapping.

Researchers are now in a race to spin the first artificial spider silk that someday may be used to create "nature's nylons."

And while we wait, ponder this: Women may hate hose, but men are apparently enamoured. Google the words "pantyhose fetish" and you'll find 3,410,000 hits.

You want 'em? You can have 'em boys. ■

1

Wearing Your Co-Worker's Pants

Imagine wearing your co-worker's pants to the office. Would you feel weird about it? How about donning their entire suit?

I had the strangest, most wonderful experience recently. And it made me rethink my lifelong obsession with clothes.

I feel good when I buy a new sweater or pair of jeans. Really good. I feel even better when the clothing I covet is on sale.

I know I'm not alone here.

If you could throw every single item of clothing you've ever worn into one pile, how big would it be? Think about it. Would it fill an 8 by 10 room? An Olympic-size swimming pool?

Imagine the mountain of discarded fashions.

The polka dotted hot pants Mom sewed me in Grade 4. Cowl neck sweaters. Those really uncomfortable rainbow-coloured socks with the individual toes. The purple turtleneck with the metal peace sign zipper. How about those corduroy overalls with the wide legs that caught fire at a bush party in 1977?

Where is that stuff now? Thirty feet down in a garbage dump?

Forgive me Mother Nature, but I can't say I miss the stuff. I've simply replaced it with other clothing items I'll probably shake my head at some day.

Luckily for me, I work in a business that lets me indulge my passion for fashion.

Problem is — I'm seriously out of room. So when a colleague proposed we hold a "bitch n' swap" party, I was intrigued.

She got the idea from a Canadian fashion magazine called Lou Lou.

It promised that this "ingenious event can help you score a red-hot wardrobe — without putting pressure on your pocketbook." Best yet, clothing items unclaimed at the end of the afternoon would go to a local women's shelter.

1

So the Global gals started digging through their closets.

The party instructions? Bring anything that's collecting dust in your closet. Clothing you're tired of — things that don't fit anymore.

The rules?

Have a glass of wine, some snacks, socialize with your colleagues and grab any clothing item on the floor that strikes your fancy. No questions asked.

OK, I had my doubts. There were 10 of us ranging in size from two to 12, including a couple of very pregnant women.

It felt… well, kind of weird manhandling my colleague's clothing. "Are you sure you want to give this dress away? Whose jeans are these? What a great necklace!"

My pile of giveaways was splayed out on an armchair in the corner. I was mildly dismayed when items were picked up, and put back down again, secretly delighted when a colleague laid something of mine on her "take-home" pile.

Turns out I wasn't the only one feeling a little angst about the process.

"My first fear was that I would bring my castoffs and nobody would want them," confessed my colleague Nicola.

"I thought I'd feel totally sad if my pile sat there untouched and lonely."

And sometimes, an old outfit magically took on a whole new look.

"I did think it was funny how you'd see something of yours that you never really liked, or never wore, and then you'd see it on someone else and it was like a totally new and beautiful shirt," my colleague Julie observed.

Me? Well, let's just say I arrived with four green garbage bags full of clothing I wasn't wearing anymore, and left with an armload of new things, including dress pants, suit jackets and sweaters. I even scored a fancy new party top.

But the real fun began the following week, when we all marched into work day after day modelling our "new" wardrobes.

"Isn't that Lesley's jacket? It looks great! Hey J'lyn — I'm wearing your hot pink sweater today. Margo, those velour sweats were so comfortable, I put them on when I got home and promptly fell asleep on the couch."

In the end, it was a win-win-win situation.

We cleaned out our closets — picked up a few new things to wear — AND donated a truckload of gently worn clothing to the WINGS shelter.

It was fun. It felt good. It's going to happen again this spring. ■

1

Hair Obsession

I'm obsessed with something that's dead.

For years I tried to torture this sorry beast into submission. Harsh chemicals — flesh-searing heat — sharp objects. Yet it still has enormous power over me. It mocks me. One day playing submissive, making me inordinately grateful. The next, being obstinate, driving me to utter despair.

To make matters worse, this petulant monster has an incessant appetite for attention. I pay its highly trained keeper upwards of $1,000 a year to keep things in check.

I'm talking about the joy and bane of every woman's existence — my hair.

I hate being controlled by something so frivolous. But to me, having a bad hair day is like nursing a festering chin pimple. It sucks a bit of the wind out of your sails — ratchets down your confidence quotient a few notches.

An old school chum met me for lunch recently. We hadn't seen each other in 20 years, so she brought an envelope full of old pictures to help grease the conversational wheels.

I tried to suppress a shriek of horror as I laid eyes on my 18-year-old self, mugging for the camera sporting a brassy fright wig of frazzled hair and clown-like cheek blush.

In my defense, it was the era of disco 'fros giving way to the big hair bands of the '80s.

Frankly, in retrospect we all looked like idiots.

Hair has played a major role in shaping our history, our ideals of beauty, and both women, and men for that matter, have long been willing to suffer for their crowning glory.

Madame de Pompadour inspired an era of ridiculousness. The mistress of Louis XV of France was known for throwing elaborate theme parties for the socialites of the French court. The website hairrific.com tells tales of artists hired to create hairstyles in keeping with the party theme, including outrageous dos containing cages with live birds inside, even miniature naval battles complete with ships and smoke.

Women of the day suffered backaches from sporting these monstrous creations. On long coach trips they had to travel with their heads between their legs because they literally couldn't bear the weight.

And forget the sweet smelling hair products of today. Back then, a popular recipe for hair pomade called for the mixing of bear grease in a pot with hazelnut oil and lemon juice.

This malodorous concoction attracted unwelcome "visitors" to the bed whilst the lady slept — prompting the old saying, "her hair's a rat's nest".

Things weren't a whole lot better by the 20th century. Hairdos were still done once a week by a professional, and meant to last several days with only minor tweaking.

Jonn Gluwchynski is owner of a popular Edmonton salon called The Cutting Room. His fascination with hair began as a little boy watching his mother's weekly pilgrimage to the salon.

"She left looking like a tired old mom, and came back like Wonder Woman. She looked taller, more beautiful, with more confidence," Jonn reminisces.

"It was like she went into a phone booth and came out a different person. That really stuck in my head — how beauty was power."

Jonn says the hair profession was vaulted into a new era in the late 1960s by a group of hairdressers in England dubbed the "Fab Five".

They introduced the Sassoon bob - a precision wash-and-wear haircut that women could manage on their own between monthly visits to the salon.

The one-named celebrity hairstyle icons followed. Farrah. Cher. Madonna.

And don't forget the guys. Brad. Lenny. Axyl. Even "The Donald" — poster boy for balding men around the world.

"There's nothing worse than the big lie of the comb-over." laments Jonn.

"Now guys are saying, 'You know what, I'm losing my hair, I'm not fooling anyone.' So they shave it off, and there's confidence in making that decision. It shows power, virility. They know who they are."

Truth be told, I guess I'm living the big lie too.

I haven't really been a blond since I was about four. ■

Makeup Mania

Don't you just love those makeover shows?

A woman with straggly dishwater hair and 1970's lipstick is whisked behind a curtain, only to emerge a couple of hours later looking like a cover girl. It's amazing what a little lip-gloss and mascara can do to boost a gal's confidence.

I love makeup, and I'll confess right here to being an extremely easy mark at the cosmetics counter.

"So it works best if you use the primer first, then the foundation, followed by the setting powder? Ok I'll take it all." Ka-ching!

I know it sounds rather vacuous, but hey - some women buy shoes when they need a lift - I buy a new lipstick. It's the never-ending shopping trip. I've spent my entire adult life looking for the perfect pinky beige lipstick that's not too frosty, not too brown, and I've got the bulging makeup bags to prove it.

So when I heard the mecca of all makeup stores was coming to Edmonton, I felt a little shiver of delight. Sephora's setting up shop here? I'm in for some serious trouble.

It's a cosmetic junkie's paradise, decked out like a Hollywood soundstage with flattering lighting, mirrors, stools, sponges, Kleenex and literally thousands of products you're encouraged to test drive at mini-makeup stations.

The sales people are called "cast members". When they're on the floor, they're "on stage", when they're in the storeroom, they're "backstage". They wear "costumes" instead of work uniforms. It's all rather theatrical, and it works.

The mirrors and lights, and row upon row of blush, eye shadow, perfume and lipstick suck you in, and before you know it, you've got half a dozen things in your little shopping basket you didn't know you needed.

I went to my first Sephora in Manhattan. I could have spent a couple of hours in there, but my husband was bored in about 10 minutes, and stood outside on the sidewalk in Times Square, waiting for me to pull myself away from the Smashbox aisle.

Same thing happened when we visited the store in Las Vegas this year. 15 minutes to peruse the products - then get your stuff and let's go. I should have married a drag queen.

1

Clearly this was meant to be a solo mission. So on a recent day off, I made my way to the big mall to check out the new Sephora outlet by myself. No time restrictions – no toe tapping spouse.

The selection was delightfully mind-boggling, 13,000 items from mimosa bubble bath, to ingrown hair eliminating peeling pads. The products even had cool names like "Tanning Bed in a Tube", "Caribbean in a Compact", and the aptly named "Hope in a Jar".

Some products were rather clever. Mini lip-glosses you attach to your cell-phone, or the eye shadow palette with the built-in voice recording giving step-by-step instructions on how to achieve the smoky eye look.

There's a ridiculously large selection of accessories designed to tweeze, squeeze, puff, buff, blow, curl, clip, file and straighten.

And lest you think the store is just for the ladies – there's a manly section too, for guys worried about razor burn, zits, baggy eyes and clogged pores. Mind you, I saw only two male customers the entire time I was in the store, and of the 41 "cast members" who work at Sephora, only one is a guy. (He's not gay – I asked.)

An hour and a half later, my shopping excursion was nearly complete and I was heading to the checkout when a stranger walked up and said, "Excuse me, I hope you don't think this is weird, but I love the perfume you're wearing, what is it?"

Uh, which one? I'd sampled at least four. This one? The woman smelled my left wrist.

"No, I don't think so."

Was it this one? I offered up my right wrist. "Nope." We both laughed.

It was fun. I spent way too much money. I'm sure I'll be back. Alone.

St. Tropez or Liver Disease?

I have a love/hate relationship with self-tanners.

I love the look of sun kissed skin. I hate the stinky, streaky products that don't quite deliver on their promises.

For one thing, the resulting colour is still more liver failure than Saint Tropez — and no one's come up with a foolproof application process yet either.

My left ankle is currently sporting a rust coloured blob — courtesy Neutrogena's new MicroMist Sunless Spray self-tanner. The back of the can says "The mist is so light and fine, the coverage so even, there's no need to rub!"

It neglects to mention the mist is so light, fine and INVISIBLE, you also can't see where it's going.

I've tried the tinted self-tanners. They leave nicotine-like stains on my french manicure.

My colleague's husband is a rural vet. He dropped off a handful of BSE surgical gloves for me to try the other day. They kept my nails from discolouring, but left a powdered residue on my legs. The residue combined with the tanning foam to create mottled streaks that now mimic a hideous skin disorder.

This may all sound rather shallow — but after decades of scorching my skin in the hot Alberta sun, I desperately need to find a believable canned tan… because it's a bloody miracle I haven't developed skin cancer yet.

We were gullible 30 years ago. We bought those TV commercials that showed beautiful people romping on beaches slathered in coconut-scented suntan oil. Being tanned was apparently for the happy and healthy — right? Wrong.

I once sat outside at a baseball tournament roasting in the 30-plus heat until I was literally sick to my stomach with sunstroke. By nightfall, I had actual blisters behind my knees, and couldn't stand up straight for the next 48 hours.

Even dumber was my old college classmate who went on a spring skiing trip. Instead of hitting the slopes, she sat at the top of the hill with one of those silver reflector boards aimed at her face, hoping to get a head start on her summer tan. What she got instead was a bona fide second-degree burn.

1

She came to school on the Monday with a puffed up face and a washcloth in her purse to blot the weeping blisters. Disgusting.

What were we thinking back then?

And whatever happened to the centuries-old notion that tans were only for peasants and labourers?

Pale skin used to indicate high society.

Women in ancient Greece and Rome were so anxious to display their social status they actually used lead paints and chalk to colour their faces white.

By the mid-10th century, arsenic was the preferred method of lightening skin tone, often with deadly consequences.

During the reign of Queen Elizabeth, women even painted thin blue lines on their foreheads to give their skin a more translucent appearance.

It wasn't until the '20s that society started associating tans with living the good life.

Fashion designer Coco Chanel was cruising from Paris to Cannes on the Duke of Wellington's yacht in 1923. By the time the boat had docked, she was sporting a dark suntan. It was quite accidental, but the press assumed Chanel was making a deliberate fashion statement.

The era of sunbathing was born.

Eighty-two years later, we're paying the price with alarming rates of skin cancer.

At least my generation had an excuse. We didn't know how dangerous the sun's rays were. It seemed perfectly reasonable to pour baby oil on your limbs and lay prone in the direct sunshine for hours at a time.

Today's teens should know better. There's all kinds of information out there about the dangers of sun exposure, and if they think they can dodge the cancer bullet they're still going to pay the price by prematurely aging their skin. Too bad sun damage didn't show up immediately in the form of big, purple facial boils. I guarantee we'd all run for cover.

So my search for the "dream-tan-in-a-can" continues.

If you've found the perfect product, do the ladies of the world a favour. Spread the word, and maybe – just maybe, you might help save someone from developing skin cancer. ■

1

Cream Dreams

For a reasonably intelligent human being, I can be pretty stupid sometimes.

I've repeatedly allowed myself to be tricked and manipulated — scammed out of hundreds, perhaps even thousands of dollars in a pathetic search for something that doesn't exist... an anti-aging cream that actually works.

They're called cosmeceuticals. That's a fancy name for a product that can make all kinds of outlandish promises it doesn't have to keep.

"A non-surgical face lift in a bottle!"

"Look 10 years younger in two weeks!"

These overpriced creams and serums are gussied up in high-tech, glossy packaging, boasting impressive sounding ingredients like hydroxyethylcellulose, and superoxide dismutase. Sounds pretty scientific to me. And look at the price — they must work!

My over-40 girlfriends are always trading tips on the latest "must-try" product on the market. One summer at our annual girls' weekend away, my normally level-headed friend Mo was gushing over the latest "miracle" skin product, a shockingly expensive face cream called Creme de la Mer.

She insisted we'd notice a difference in under-eye bags and crows feet within minutes.

So, as we sipped our morning coffee on the deck in our pyjamas, Mo played beautician, flitting from one woman to another, dabbing her precious Creme de la Mer around our puffy too-much-wine-last-night eyes. She then snapped "before and after" digital photos so we could see the difference for ourselves.

Ah the power of persuasion.

Hope overriding doubt, we excitedly agreed that, "I really DO see a difference! Look the puffiness is gone!"

Was Creme de la Mer finally the real deal? Incredible! It costs how much? Unbelievable. Doubt begins to creep back in. But just look at the results...

When I got back home, I rushed straight to the beauty counter at Holt's and

---

1

bought my own little pot of gold. I could hardly wait to recreate the dramatic age-defying effects from the girl's weekend.

So I patted the cream onto my eyes and waited. And waited. Several minutes passed by. I stared intently into the bathroom mirror looking for signs of an anti-aging miracle. Nope. The under-eye bags were still there. So were the crow's feet. Argghhh… I'm such an idiot.

I take slight comfort in knowing I'm not alone.

Debra Scheufler is a 47-year-old lawyer from San Diego who filed a class action suit against Estee Lauder, owner of the Creme de la Mer brand.

Scheufler had tried the pricey cream for about four months, and says not only did it NOT make her look younger as advertised, it actually clogged up her pores. She looked up the ingredients in the dictionary and discovered a key component in Creme de la Mer was petrolatum (read Vaseline).

So Scheufler sued, claiming Estee Lauder was guilty of false advertising. She wants all unsatisfied customers to be reimbursed up to $1,500. Good luck.

Canadians will spend over five billion dollars on cosmeceuticals this year. Intellectually we know there's no such thing as a facelift in a bottle, so why do we continue to buy these blatantly false promises?

"Because we want them to be true."

Paula Begoun is author of several best-selling books on the beauty industry, including *Don't Go to the Cosmetics Counter Without Me.*

"We want these products to work, and it's worth the money and eventual disappointment to see if the next claim might be true."

Begoun says there are lots of good products out there, but none live up to their dramatic claims, and she warns that expensive does not necessarily mean better.

Consumer Reports recently put anti-wrinkle creams to the test, and found no correlation between effectiveness and price. In fact, the Olay Regenerist product line was rated as "slightly more effective" than products six times the price point. But even the Olay line was found to provide a less than 10-percent reduction of wrinkles when researchers studied the skin with high-tech optical devices.

Take heart though, there is some good news to report on the anti-aging front.

The experts all agree there's one inexpensive product on the market guaranteed to hold back the hands of time.

It's called sunscreen. ■

1

The Trout Pout

What's up with society's fixation with full lips? And who decided that bigger is better anyway?

Angelina Jolie is making life hell for all of us thin-lipped gals in the world.

People magazine recently named her the Most Beautiful Woman in the World for 2006. There's no doubt she's stunning with her dramatic blue-green eyes and perfect bone structure, but it's that mouth that gets most of the attention. If Pamela's the poster girl for fake boobs, then Angelina's the pinup for pucker power.

And she may be the only Hollywood actress who can lay claim to that title without a little help from Dr. Feel Good and his syringe full of cow collagen.

Did you catch that recent Dynasty reunion TV special? Actress Linda Evans was almost unrecognizable with her face stretched back behind her ears, and her lips inflated to cartoonish proportions.

America's sweetheart Meg Ryan was ridiculed for denying her lip-enhancement surgery. Instead of making her more alluring, most men I know thought her new "trout pout" was a turnoff.

Edmonton dermatologist Dr. Don Groot is seeing a steady increase in the number of patients looking for lip-enhancement procedures.

"I think it's because of Angelina Jolie. We see people coming in for a real sort of bee-stung appearance, but most are opting for a more natural fullness of the lips."

Let's be honest here. Achieving the "natural" look requires undergoing some rather "unnatural" procedures like having synthetic beads injected into the lips, or Gore-Tex strips permanently implanted. Some women have collagen culled from cow skin or human cadavers injected into their mouths. Now that's sexy. Others opt to have their own fat sucked out of nether regions and transferred to their lips.

A thin-lipped pal of mine chose the latter, saying it just seemed more "natural." She was not prepared for what happened next.

"The doctor held my head with one hand and inserted this knitting needle-sized tube into the outer corner of my mouth," my friend laments. "There was an audible ripping sound as the needle tore flesh to the centre of my mouth. This was repeated on the other side. I lay there sobbing with an ice pack on my lips."

The procedure cost $600. The desired effects lasted exactly three weeks.

After hearing that story, I can honestly say I've never been tempted. Sure, I've wasted money on those cinnamon-spiced lip potions that claim to plump your lips to twice their normal size. My lips felt bigger because they were inflamed and uncomfortable, but they looked exactly the same.

If it's not shrivelling lip lines, it's crow's feet, weight-loss woes or cellulite. You name the obsession — there's a product or procedure on the market to address it.

What kind of message does that send to the next generation?

A friend of mine recently directed a show for cable television about a woman undergoing lip enhancement and breast augmentation. During the filming, the patient's daughters spoke often about their own flaws, and said they wouldn't hesitate to undergo plastic surgery themselves. That's just sad.

It's my friend Mo's favourite rant these days. "What about global warming, Darfur, the president of Iran threatening to blow us all to kingdom come?" she rages. "Let's give our daughters real, valuable role models. Let them see us obsessing about the state of the world they must inherit, rather than the puffiness of our lips."

Oddly enough, one of those role models could well be the Hollywood actress who has chosen to devote much of her time, profile and wealth to helping the world's less fortunate as a UNICEF goodwill ambassador — that luscious-lipped humanitarian Angelina Jolie. ■

Custom Fit personal trainer Jeff Woods puts Lynda through the paces — Photo courtesy: Shaughn Butts

Treadmills & Trainers

I used to think personal trainers were only for the very rich, very lazy, or very bored.

Really, who needs a high-priced babysitter in the gym? Not me.

My fitness motto? No fooling around. No chatting. No talking on the cellphone. Get in. Get out. Hit the shower. Head to work.

But after years of five days a week at the gym, I'm admittedly just going through the motions, and the belly bulge over my jeans is distressing.

I recently had my body fat analysed at a new facility called the Body Composition Clinic. It uses low dose dual X-ray technology to scan your body and calculate your overall fat percentage.

The verdict?

My bones weigh exactly four and a half pounds. I have 92 pounds worth of muscle and 32 pounds of fat. That's 24.9 per cent of my total body weight. Not bad. I squeaked into the clinic's "fitness" range for women, two levels up from "obese".

But barely fit is not good enough. So I broke down and hired a personal trainer twice a week. His name is Jeff Woods, co-owner of a popular downtown gym called Custom Fit.

"I think many people are motivated, but typically they go into the gym and they do the same program they've been doing for years."

Jeff is one of the personal trainers featured in the hit reality series Taking it Off.

He's seen a lot of would-be athletes like me who are keen to succeed, but don't have the proper fitness education.

"They're selling themselves short. They don't vary the intensity a great deal so there's a large percentage of people who don't see results when they work out on their own."

Jeff spent our first session evaluating my overall fitness level.

The workout was a bit of a blur, but I recall doing a little cardio, some circus-like gyrations on the exercise ball, and exactly twelve squats.

Big deal, right? The next day at work I sounded like a Russian power lifter every time I stood up from my desk.

Early on I confessed to Jeff that I secretly desired a… shall we say, "more defined" gluteus maximus. Not J.Lo- sized, just small "b" bootylicious.

I quickly found myself lunging around the gym like a madwoman. A squat here, a squat there… say goodbye to your flat derriere!

In a stroke of good luck, my friend Jonn Gluwchynski works out at exactly the same time with his personal trainer.

"I am in search of the elusive abs," Jonn confesses.

"I've been told they're there, and occasionally I think I can feel them, but I'm still not seeing them in the mirror. I'm going to do whatever it takes."

Funny isn't it? We're both pining for something that starts with an "a" and ends with an "s".

I've tried to maintain a shred of dignity during my personal training sessions. A dab of lip gloss, a touch of mascara. By the end of the hour I've morphed into a fuchsia-faced dishrag muttering "I don't normally sweat this much… really, it's just so unusual!"

Apparently I've been pretty much wasting my time at the gym in the past, and I'm a busy person, I hate wasting my time. So I'm turning into a huge believer in the personal trainer concept.

Sure it's expensive, but it's an investment in your health and well-being, right?

"I definitely never worked as hard as I do now," Jonn admits.

"I'm drenched and exhausted when I leave the gym. I give it 110 per cent… and maybe that's the cheap Polack coming out in me, but I want to make sure I'm getting my full money's worth."

Even if Jonn never gets his much-coveted abs, Jeff says the benefits provided by a personal trainer are undeniable.

"You'll always end up improving your cardio/respiratory health by virtue of exercising, and not always will we see some of the changes in the mirror — but there are all kinds of intrinsic benefits for sure."

Forget Jonn. What about me? Will I ever get the glorious glutes I so desire?

"Yes, by doing the right exercises, I think that potential exists.' " Jeff says. (It must be noted this is delivered with some hesitation.)

Clearly I'll never have Beyonce's butt, but I sure wish I had her money.

If I did, I'd hire Jeff five days a week. ■

1

Domestically Challenged

I'm starting a new support group for women who either aren't inclined, or don't have the time to be domestic divas. It's called TAMMONA. The Anti-Martha Movement of North America.

You can join by answering the following five questions:

1. Do you own a full or partial set of china?

2. Have you ever baked a pie from scratch?

3. Do you own any of the following appliances?

   a) food processor b) crock pot c) blender d) coffee bean grinder

4. Is someone paid to clean your house?

5. Have you hosted a dinner party in the past three months?

Give yourself one point for each question you answered "yes", and a bonus point if you own all four appliances in question number three.

If your total score is four or higher, I applaud you. I admire you. I envy you.

If your score is four or higher AND you have children, I bow down in the presence of domestic greatness. But, — you are not qualified to join TAMMONA.

This is a support group for women who'd rather stick a fork in their eye than spend a Saturday afternoon whipping up a batch of homemade cookies, or defrosting the freezer.

Cooking bores me. I don't like following recipes. I have no idea which herb goes with what.

When we have guests over, I want to be in the living room drinking wine and laughing, not stuck in the kitchen chopping onions or setting the table.

If I can't toast it, nuke it or grill it... I'm not interested. My husband and I eat out. A lot.

1

Laundry? Years ago an old boyfriend asked me to throw in a load of his dirty clothes. I'm lousy at math but I've learned this equation: 1 red hockey jersey + 4 pairs of white skivvies = powder pink briefs. Oops.

My house plants are the non-watering silk variety. I've planted an outdoor garden once in my life. The neighbour came outside and applauded.

I can't sew, either. If a hem falls down, I've been known to use duct tape to hold it up until I can drop it off at the tailors.

It's not that I'm lazy. I just don't care about this stuff. It's domestic drudgery, and I have other things I'd rather do when I'm not at work… like talk to my husband, go to the gym, read a book, do volunteer work, phone friends, go shopping, or nap.

I work as hard as any man. I contribute an equal amount to the family income. I'm no Betty Crocker waiting in the kitchen with a checkered apron and a red lipsticked smile to attend to my husband's every need.

I'm tired when I get home. I don't have the energy to pamper someone else. I'm trying to chill out, and get ready for the next day at work. So why do I feel this niggling guilt about shirking my "domestic duties?"

My husband is a saint. He never complains. He's happy to eat out several times a week. He does his own laundry and irons like a pro. He's perfectly capable of taking care of himself.

Does he wish he had a doting wife who was equal parts gourmet cook, maid and masseuse? Probably. But he knew what he was getting into when he married me — a career woman who finds cooking and cleaning tedious.

You know what? Forget the support group. We both need a wife. ■

Lori Mitchell, President Tomboy Tools Canada

Tomboy Tools

When I was in grade six, the boys took shop, and the girls took Home Ec. What a sexist rip off.

The guys had fun building birdhouses, while we got stuck baking stuffed apples and sewing corduroy ponchos. No wonder I swing a hammer like a girl.

In fact, I didn't own a single tool when I moved into my first apartment. I had to rely on boyfriends to do any fixer-upper type projects.

The first time I used a power tool was last summer at a Habitat for Humanity event that was teaching women how to build homes for low-income families. I felt both tentative and euphoric. LOOK AT ME USING A POWER SAW! I nearly pounded my chest and grunted with pleasure.

You see - I've spent my entire married life deferring to my husband when it comes to anything that requires the use of a hand tool. He's a handy guy, but he's also incredibly busy, and if I want the stripped faucet in the bathroom fixed, he usually has 800 other things on his priority list that trump minor home repairs.

Sound familiar?

Women are sick of waiting on men to get the job done. So, inspired by countless TV home renovation shows, they're strapping on their tool belts in record numbers and smashing down walls, laying tile, and installing new shelving units.

"A sense of empowerment really does come from taking control of the situation you're facing in your own home."

Lori Mitchell is president of a company that's cashing in on women's growing obsession with home renovation.

Tomboy Tools Canada hosts home based parties catering to women who want to release their inner designer divas. Instead of eyeballing the latest Tupperware product line, the ladies sip wine, and test-drive female-friendly tools. Like a self-loading hammer with a specially weighted handle that lets you drive a nail into a piece of wood with a single stroke. Or how about a 9.6 volt lightweight power drill with an angled grip designed for a woman's smaller hand?

"This woman came up and picked up our drill and was drilling into the board when she started to cry."

Lori was alarmed at first, until the woman in her 50's explained that when she first tried to use a drill as a 20 year old, she didn't know she needed to put a bit in the end. No one had told her.

"The sense of empowerment was so overwhelming, she broke down in tears over it."

Lori says single women make up the fastest growing segment of home buyers in North America, and women who live with a spouse or boyfriend are still responsible for 90 per cent of the decisions made around home improvement.

Think about it. Who picks the paint colours? We do. The guys have to agree of course… but really, for the most part, they could care less between Benjamin Moore's milk chocolate #42 and mocha #48, as long as the bedroom doesn't end up Barbie's hot pink #6.

And women are not stopping at home renovation. Alberta's hot economy has many companies in desperate need of skilled tradesmen… or women.

In 1999, NAIT had a combined total of 274 women enrolled in the trades programs. In 2006/2007, that number exploded to 816.

A record number of women have signed up for the electrician program at NAIT this year. 14 women are in their first year of training, and nine in the second year, making up 10 per cent of the students in each of those classes. Normally women make up only one to two per cent of the students in that program.

A program called Women Building Futures is also making news, training low-income Alberta women - many of them victims of domestic abuse - for jobs in the trades. 170 graduates have already found work in the construction industry, enjoying high pay and job security.

The program also runs regular home reno and repair workshops called The Fixit Chicks. Women learn everything from how to fix a leaky toilet to basic car repairs.

Wow. We've come a long way from learning how to bake stuffed apples in Home Ec.

It's about bloody time. ■

1

It's A Man's World

(Lynda's husband Norm, Mom Thelma, Lynda and Dad Dennis)

Dad's & Daughters

This is an early Father's Day message to all you men out there who have daughters.

Whether they're four or 40, they'll always be your little girl, and you should never underestimate the impact you have on their lives.

Dr. Linda Nielsen is a professor at Wake University in the States, and an expert in adolescent psychology.

She's worked with daughters both young and old for over 30 years and says, "Regardless of their age, daughters who have meaningful, comfortable relationships with their fathers are generally more self-confident and independent, have better relationships with men, are less depressed, have fewer eating disorders, drug or alcohol problems, and achieve more in school and at work."

The father-daughter bond is powerful and often heartbreakingly wonderful.

2

My Dad used to call me Lulu when I was a little girl. He still does actually, and it melts my heart every time.

When I was very small, he was your typical '60s dad… more focused on bringing home a paycheque than the toddlers back home.

That changed when I was 17.

One day Dad showed up at my work and took me out for a surprise lunch.

He wore his sunglasses inside the restaurant and choked back tears, as he talked about how he wished he'd spent more time with me as I was growing up and said he didn't want to waste any more time getting to know each other.

I was astounded, and profoundly touched. It was the beginning of a special relationship that gets sweeter by the year.

I asked my girlfriends to tell me about their relationships with their dads, and the responses made me cry.

"He is the most important man in my life," J'lyn told me.

"He's the first man I fell in love with. Everyone else has had to compare. He can still make his little 34-year-old girl melt, by kissing me on the nose."

My friend Kathy can relate.

"Where do I start? I am SUCH a daddy's girl. I asked him to marry me when I was five. He couldn't understand it when I felt incompetent, or ugly or unpopular. He always saw me as pretty and perfect and capable. What will I do when he is gone? Good grief, I'm crying."

My friend Franca's dad was an Italian immigrant who spent six years as a prisoner of war before moving to southern Alberta. He was delighted when his youngest daughter landed a job at the local radio station.

"When I got home he was like a giggly schoolboy. He led me into the kitchen where my mom was waiting and presented me with a box. Inside was a navy blue blazer and skirt. My dad said 'It's your first business suit."

Franca started to cry.

"That was more than 21 years ago. The suit doesn't fit anymore… I don't work in media anymore, my papa's not around anymore, but I still have the suit tucked away in my special trunk… and whenever I feel the need to be close to my Dad I just hold it in my arms. Thanks Papa for making me feel so special."

OK, now I'm crying.

I think you get the point. Daughters love their dads. Daughters "need" their dads. Always and forever.

Whether it's power washing the outside of my house, giving me financial advice, or just lending a compassionate ear when life has thrown me a curve ball, my Dad is always there for me.

He's kind, gentle, intelligent, funny, hardworking, generous and community minded. And best of all? Dad loves me unconditionally. This I know for sure.

Have a wonderful Father's Day, Dad.

Love, Lulu. ■

2

Why Men Don't Read

Women read fiction — men read magazines.

OK, "some" men read novels, but most read non-fiction, manuals, information texts, and newspapers — but novels? Not so much.

Why is that?

"Fiction doesn't appeal to me," shrugs a male colleague.

"I can't sit still long enough to read a book," another male friend explains.

"It's not exciting enough. In sports you're cheering for a team. If you're reading a book — you're just reading a book."

Interesting.

My husband likes to read about business, world leaders and health. He buys Time and Maclean's. But a novel? Nope. No interest.

This intrigues me. Most women I know love to read fiction. We swap books and share tips on hot authors and new novels. Reading is a delicious and decadent way to spend an afternoon.

Guys think it's a waste of time, and they certainly wouldn't be interested in getting together as a group to analyze the latest Oprah book club pick.

"I'd rather get together and play poker," opines a male friend. "There's a stigma associated with book clubs — you have to share your feelings."

God forbid. There's clearly a gender divide when it comes to reading.

Heather Blair is a professor in the faculty of education at the University of Alberta. She says boys and girls talk, write and read differently.

Girls are more in touch with their emotions; they like to read and write about feelings, fears and hardships in their lives.

Professor Blair says boys prefer "action, adventure, sports, racing, science fiction and fantasy." They're drawn to non-fiction, and are more computer literate than their female classmates, doing much of their reading online.

2

Boys may be forced to read novels in school, but once they graduate and have the freedom to read what they want, they often skip the fiction aisle at Chapters.

It's estimated only 20 per cent of the novels sold worldwide are bought by men. And the number of male readers is on the decline.

A Statistics Sweden report found that one in three men between the ages of 16 and 84 admit to never reading novels. When it comes to unskilled male manual workers, 46 per cent say they don't read at all. Isn't that sad?

What if they could read, drink beer and watch football with the guys at the same time? Aha! Now we're talking.

A group of guys in Virginia has found a way to combine a love of "fine" literature with a more traditionally male pastime. The Charlottesville Men's Book Club meets during halftime of Monday Night Football games.

OK, so their book selection includes titles like *Why Do Men Have Nipples?* and *I May Be Wrong But I Doubt It*, but hey — they're reading.

Oprah's doing her part to entice more men to read. Some of her recent book-club selections have featured memoirs by men.

Interestingly, the only two scandals associated with Winfrey's televised book club have involved male authors — from James Frey's public admission that he fabricated sections of *A Million Little Pieces* to Jonathan Franzen's ill-advised comment that being picked for Oprah's book club somehow tainted his novel *The Corrections*.

Oprah promptly withdrew her invitation, which sent Franzen into a back pedalling, apologetic frenzy.

But Oprah's not deterred. Her latest book-club selection is *The Road*, by the notoriously press shy and reclusive male author Cormac McCarthy. It's a post-apocalyptic novel about a father and son travelling through a barren post-nuclear landscape.

Maybe more novels written by men — about men — that get mass media attention will convince more guys to put down their magazines and pick up books.

Schools have to do their part by acknowledging the gender differences when it comes to literacy, and offering more books and reading materials that appeal to boys.

And dads have a big role to play too. Take time to sit down and read to your son.

Don't let women have all the fun when it comes to enjoying great literature. ■

Dad's Day At The Spa

Men need to learn how to chill out.

They're so busy making big corporate deals, raking the leaves or driving the kids to hockey practice, they don't take time for themselves.

Women have pretty much got the pampering concept down pat. Is there anything more delicious than a pedicure? All snuggled up in a white fluffy robe, with soft music playing in the background as someone gently massages your feet? Ahhh… heaven.

The other day I dropped a pen at a male colleague's feet.

As I bent down to pick it up, I found myself eyeball to toenail with a Halloween horror show.

"Oh, my God, your feet are hideous!" I blurted out.

His toes were covered in ginger hair, and crowned with thick, gnarly toenails, the colour of banana pudding.

This was a middle-aged man in serious need of a pedicure. When I suggested it, he looked aghast and insisted he didn't have the time, and besides, what was wrong with his toenails anyway? Pretty much everything, my friend, unless you have a fungus fetish.

I don't buy the argument that men don't have time to pamper themselves. Hey, we're all busy these days, you have to "make" time.

"They seem to feel guilty doing it."

Ed Kilbride is owner of Edmonton's first exclusively male spa, The Boardroom.

"Alberta males are still coming around to the whole idea of going to a place where you put on a robe and let someone else look after your fingers or toes."

But attitudes are changing. A survey done this year by the KSL Resorts group found that over 73 per cent of men believe spa treatments can help relieve the stress of business travel. More than 60 per cent believe spa treatments lead to an improved sex life.

2

Maybe that explains an increase in the number of men requesting sensitive waxing procedures.

"Hair is the enemy to the young male," Kilbride chuckles.

Edmonton men are waxing everything from their eyebrows to their nether regions these days. Get this — they're even requesting bikini and Brazilian wax jobs. Ouch.

There's even a new shaver on the market, made by Philips: the Bodygroom, specifically designed to shave the wobbly bits. If you've got the time and a sense of humour, check out the company's irreverent website at www.shaveeverywhere.com.

High-end hotels are also reaching out to the largely untapped male market by offering spa services with macho names like the Mountain Man's Facial, Love Handle Wrap, or Brewmaster's Choice.

The Fairmont hotel chain says men now make up 50 per cent of their spa clientele during peak times like ski season in Banff or golf season in Scottsdale, Arizona.

Interestingly, men have different desires when it comes to spa services. For one thing, unlike women, they're not keen on the relaxation massage. Most men prefer a therapeutic or deep tissue massage, and they don't feel comfortable with a male masseur, either.

While women are OK with the concept of bumping into other women at a spa, men prefer complete privacy.

Women think it's decadent to spend an hour and a half enjoying a spa pedicure. Men are all about efficiency. Fifty per cent of guys surveyed by KSL Resorts said they would choose shorter treatments — say 25 minutes — versus the traditional 50 and 90-minute spa treatments.

Guys are not only warming to the idea of waxing and manicures, they're now asking for dermatological procedures. The American Academy of Facial Plastic and Reconstructive Surgery reports a stunning 497-per-cent increase in the number of men using injectibles like Botox or collagen last year.

The Boardroom spa in downtown Edmonton is hoping to cash in on that trend. Starting in December, it's expanding the menu to include services like laser hair removal, microdermabrasion and Botox injections.

It's good to see more men taking the time to pamper and primp. They deserve it.

Ladies, why don't we help our men discover the joy of guilt-free relaxation? Let's get the guys a pedicure gift certificate for Christmas.

And if they don't use it? Well, we couldn't let it go to waste, could we? ■

2

(Gord Steinke, Eskimos kicker Sean Fleming, Eskimos wide receiver Ed Hervey, and Lynda)

Athletes & Emotion

Guys get a raw deal from society when it comes to showing emotion and affection for one another in public.

If they cry, they're accused of being wussies.

If they hug — or god forbid kiss — people question their sexuality.

So often, guys are reduced to that macho gripped-fist, shoulder-bump kind of greeting with their male friends.

It seems to be a North American hang-up.

In Thailand, men hold hands with each other. In Russia, guys kiss each other on the lips.

Here, one of the only places men are allowed to shed their inhibitions is the professional sports arena.

"I think most of us are seriously deprived of healthy touching."

Dr. Billy Strean is associate professor of physical education and recreation at the University of Alberta, and a specialist in sports psychology.

"When we're participating in something like a sports event where we have a greater amount of emotional and personal investment than in much of life, we have more emotion to show."

Hockey players hug after goals. Football players slap each other on the butt.

Remember that Spanish soccer player who was so excited after his mate scored a big goal, he leapt on the guy and nipped him on the crotch in full view of the media hordes?

OK, that was a bit weird, but as a woman, it's fun to see men get a chance to be joyous and uninhibited.

"I get so excited when I score, that hugging the guys is not enough," laughs former Oilers' enforcer Georges Laraque.

At six foot three and 255 pounds, Laraque's a tough guy who's not afraid to show emotion.

Number 27's signature move? Launching himself at the Plexiglas after scoring a goal.

"I have so much energy after I score, it helps me loosen up. Then I go hug the guys. I don't know why I get so excited."

Laraque's a friendly giant who insists on hugging women when he's introduced, because he thinks a handshake's too formal.

This big man's not afraid to show affection to his male friends either.

Georges once made a bet with a former junior hockey teammate in Quebec as they were vying for the Memorial Cup in the mid-nineties.

Their team, the Granby Predateurs, had zero chance of winning, so Laraque threw out a challenge to his hockey pal.

"I said if we win the cup we have to kiss each other on the lips while holding the cup." Laraque confesses with a big smile.

"We won the cup, and we did (kiss), and I have the picture at home."

Georges shares a jersey number with another popular Edmonton sports star, former Eskimos linebacker Singor Mobley.

Unlike Laraque, Mobley says he's not a "touchy-feely" kind of guy in day to day life. That changes when he hits the gridiron.

"We're very emotional. There's a lot of chest bumping and helmet slapping."

What about the bum slapping football's so famous for?

"We actually talked about it as a team. There's a one-second rule. You know, it's gotta be a quick slap on the butt," Mobley grins. "You can't just leave your hand sitting there for awhile."

And while there's ecstasy in victory as the sports cliche goes, there's also agony in defeat.

"Yeah guys do cry," admits Singor.

"Especially when you're in the big games, and you know you gave everything you had on the line and you come up short. Your emotions do take over."

Mobley admits to shedding a few tears during the team's Grey Cup loss to Montreal on home turf in 2002 — frustration that turned to elation when they avenged their loss the following year.

But no matter how big the game — how sweet the victory — there's a limit to all that hugging and bum slapping. The intimacy ends at the locker room door.

"Never, never do you touch a guy naked," warns Laraque. "Not even with your pinky finger on his shoulder. It's like an unwritten rule."

Singor Mobley says the same taboo exists in pro football.

"Once you get off the field the emotion is gone. The excitement — it's all over with, and it's like an off and on switch. As soon as you go back to the locker-room you go back to normal life. So don't hug me — don't smack me on the butt type of deal."

Oh well, it may be fleeting — but at least for a few moments each year, "real" men are allowed to be real. ∎

Co-anchors Gord Steinke, Lynda & Claire Martin at Commonwealth Stadium for the Heritage Classic

Hockey Fever

Are you sick of hockey yet?

Bored to tears with the excessive media coverage? Annoyed by the twit who sits across from you at work wearing his Pronger jersey on game days?

Well get over yourself.

I know hockey's an acquired taste. Not everyone's interested, and that's OK, but this is not an IQ test. Hockey fans are every bit as educated as you are. It's not a badge of honour to pooh-pooh the playoffs, mocking the millions of Canadians who do enjoy the game.

You're entitled to your opinion, but I dare say people who aren't fans of the sport don't really understand it and haven't considered the spin-off factors that benefit us all.

So to help ease your discomfort, here are my top 10 reasons to watch the Stanley Cup playoffs.

1. The Thrill of Competition.

It's fast, it's physical, it's a three-hour white-knuckle couch ride. The game is equal measures finesse, hard work, passion and luck. Just when you think your team has it in the bag, a bad bounce swings the momentum in favor of the opponents. In the playoffs, it ain't over till it's over baby.

2. Hometown Pride

For years, the American teams with fatter budgets and bigger arenas outspent the small market Canadian teams, buying the Cup with high priced talent. The Oilers are proving the "New NHL" has leveled the playing field. The game is fun again, may the best team win —- not the highest paid roster.

3. Edmonton Profile

Fifteen years ago while shooting a documentary in Ukraine, some rural sausage makers were delighted to learn I was from Edmonton. "Wayne Gretzky! Edmonton Oilers!" they beamed at me. These guys couldn't speak English, but they sure knew their hockey. It took a while, but in 2006, the international spotlight is once again shining brightly on the City of Champions.

4. Economic Impact

In the first round of the playoffs, each home game was worth $1 million to the Oilers organization. Round two — $1.2 million. Round three — $1.4 million. That's not counting the beer and merchandise sales.

I've met many people who've travelled to Edmonton to soak up the playoff atmosphere and spend their hard earned dollars here.

5. Venus and Mars

Hockey is not exclusively a guy's sport. Women love it too. It's a perfect way to spend time with your man, or maybe get to know your male colleagues a little better. Hockey is the great equalizer. Gender is not a factor when it comes to being a great fan.

6. Hero Worship

In a time of global conflict — wars, death, crime, drugs — we could use a few more heroes. The guys in copper and blue have demonstrated class, passion, skill, teamwork and an impressive work ethic.

7. The Global Village

Few things can unite strangers from a town, city, province or country like a Canadian team vying for the Stanley Cup playoffs. It's a common bond, a point of pride, a reason to rally together for a common goal. Even some Flames fans are jumping on the Oilers bandwagon.

8. Athletic Excellence

In the Stanley Cup playoffs, good players working toward a common goal become great players. The team is everything. Guts equal glory. Success breeds confidence, which fosters belief, and when you truly believe, anything is possible. It's a life lesson we can all learn from.

9. The Sum of the Parts

The "team" is number one, but when you become a fan of the game, you come to know a little more about the individual hearts beating beneath the jerseys. Like the gritty captain nicknamed "Gator" who leads with his passion and work ethic. Or the pride and joy of little Italy — Fernando Pisani, an Edmonton kid who grew up watching the team on TV because he couldn't afford a ticket to the game.

10. Hockey Heritage

Bottom line — it's our game. Canada made it great. We have the history. The best players in the NHL are usually from Canada. We have the loudest, most passionate, best-educated fans.

Enough said. If I still haven't convinced you... your loss.

To all the true hockey fans out there... Go Oilers Go! ■

Rumours In Cyberspace

Pssssst.

Wanna know the real reason behind star defenseman Chris Pronger's abrupt departure from Edmonton? I'll tell you what I know in a minute.

But first, how about that jungle pipeline?

My god the rumours have been flying. Friends and former colleagues are e-mailing from Calgary, Ottawa, Vancouver, Washington, DC.

"What's up with this Chris Pronger story? I've heard he…" blah, blah, blah.

Remember that old game you played as a kid where the first person whispered a story to the next person, then they told the person sitting next to them, and so on until the last person in line had to repeat the story aloud? It was always a hilarious, skewed version of the original.

The Internet is creating a split second, international game of he-said, she-said in cyberspace, where people who hide behind web monikers like Rocketman and Foxygirl spread salacious, often malicious gossip about people they've never met.

It's like pouring gasoline down a back alley and tossing a match. POOF! The lies and half-truths explode and race through cyberspace, often crossing international borders.

Someone reads a juicy tidbit on a web thread, then repeats the gossip to the guy at the lunch counter, who goes back to work and tells his colleagues, who then e-mail friends and family members, and before you know it, the rumour is "fact". And unlike that trail of flaming gasoline, with the Internet, it's impossible to trace the original source. No one has to own up to the rumour. No one has to offer up proof. Anonymous people can say whatever they want about whomever they want, no matter how damaging and nasty.

There's been a backroom debate in media circles about the whole Chris Pronger incident. How come no one has the guts to dig up the real story and go on record with it?

The problem with that is twofold. First, you damn well better have your facts right and be able to prove it, or get sued. Secondly, you have to ask yourself, whose business is it anyway?

2

A colleague was ranting about the rumours the other day, insisting that Pronger has no choice but to come clean and put an end to the hurtful gossip.

And it has been hurtful. The fans are hurt, angry and confused. The Oilers are hurting, after losing a superstar they were building the team around. Chris Pronger and his family have been hurt. Worse yet, innocent people have been hurt.

Here's what I know about the Chris Pronger affair.

I know he could have handled his trade request more graciously.

If I were his agent, I would have advised him to issue a statement before he left Edmonton that went something like this:

"I would like to say thank you to the Oilers organization and my teammates for the most successful and enjoyable season of my career."

"Thanks also, to the great fans that supported me. Edmonton is an incredible hockey city — the best in the league. I enjoyed my time here, but for personal reasons that I am not prepared to discuss, I now feel it is in the best interests of my family to request a trade."

"I wish the Oilers continued success. Playing in Edmonton will always be one of the highlights of my career."

That wouldn't have silenced all the boo-birds, but it would have helped assuage the feelings of fans insulted that maybe Edmonton wasn't good enough for the hockey star and his family.

In the end, we're left with nothing but rumours, and the truth is, we may never know the "real" story behind Chris Pronger's trade request, and maybe that's the way it should be.

Six months from now, the Internet rumour mill will be churning out a new titillating tale involving some other high profile figure, and we'll forget all about Chris Pronger's unfortunate departure from Edmonton.

That is until the first time he steps foot on the ice at Rexall Place dressed like a Duck.

A sitting duck. ■

Welcome to Edmonton

I often find myself defending Edmonton to people who think the city is a frozen wasteland of strip malls, fast food outlets and blue-collar workers.

Edmonton has been getting a bum rap for years, and I'm sick of it. The negativity is not fair, and it doesn't help when millionaire athletes are leery of moving here because they don't think it's cosmopolitan enough for their families. Thanks for nothing Chris Pronger.

So it's a bit ironic that our newest defensive superstar is also pulling on the number 44 jersey after signing another five-year mega contract worth millions. Who is this Sheldon Souray guy anyway? Does he really plan on sticking around for the long haul? The mother of his children is a former Baywatch actress who lives in LA. He's a good- looking young guy who's modeled for GQ magazine. Ding, ding, ding…as a jilted Oilers fan, my alarm bells are ringing.

I wanted to talk to this guy myself. So I asked the Oilers for an interview, and Souray agreed, calling me on his cell phone as he drove to a hockey school program in the LA area recently. Now that he's had time to absorb the idea of living in Edmonton what does he think?

"I'm excited about it," enthused the new Oilers star.

Really?

"It's been a dream of mine forever to play for the Oilers. It's nothing but exciting."

Hmm. I guess growing up in Elk Point, Alberta puts a different spin on things.

That and the fact his immediate family still lives in the Edmonton area. But it's been 16 years since Souray played junior hockey for the Fort Saskatchewan Traders, what does he think of Edmonton now?

"I guess Dorothy was right when she said there's no place like home."

Sheldon Souray says the city is bigger than he remembers it, but the people have not changed. They're open, friendly and supportive. The 31 year-old says in other major cities he's played in, if you say good morning to someone in a coffee shop, they look at you suspiciously wondering what you want.

2

"In Edmonton, you say good morning to someone, and you have to look at your watch five minutes later and be polite about getting out of the conversation." Souray laughs.

I think he's nailed it. Edmonton's greatest asset is the people who live here.

We are a big city with a small town folksiness that's charming. Strangers still smile and say hello when they pass each other on the bike paths. If disaster strikes, Edmontonians come to the rescue, displaying incredible generosity. When a major sporting event is held here, Edmontonians are proud, and show up by the ten's of thousands. We have a reputation for volunteering that is unparalleled in the country, and when Edmonton throws a party, whether it's the World Games, or the province's centennial, we do it up right.

Our river valley is spectacular year round, from the crisp green of spring, to the mango yellow of fall – even the fresh white blanket of winter is beautiful.

The downtown is flourishing, with cranes dotting the skyline, a growing, healthy bustle of people on the sidewalks, and world class restaurants and shopping.

Edmonton has internationally renowned universities and colleges, plus a network of medical facilities and professionals that have made us the envy of North America.

And when it comes to sports, the City of Champions has it all - home to world class figure skaters, Olympic athletes, and great sporting dynasties in the Eskimos and Oilers.

And that brings us back to Sheldon Souray.

So far he's saying all the right things about settling down in Edmonton. But is he going to get here, play one year and then pull a Chris Pronger?

"I've never in my career asked for a trade, I'm not that kind of guy." Souray insists.

"I want to help these guys go all the way in five years. Hopefully not once, but a couple of times."

Now we're talking.

Welcome to Edmonton Sheldon. Hope you enjoy your stay. ■

(Millwoods golf pro Darrell McDonald gives Lynda her first golf lesson)

Foreplay

Did you know that golf is better than sex? That some guys would rather be celibate than told they could never hit the links again in their life?

Wow.

I work with a guy who's an avid — no make that borderline obsessive — golfer. He spends thousands of dollars on green fees, and says he would golf every day of his life if he could.

When asked if he had to make a choice — never have sex again or never play golf again — he quickly chose celibacy, saying "I went without sex for seven years and it was no big deal."

This is intriguing to me. I've pretended to play golf about three times in my life. It was kinda fun, but better than sex? I'm clearly missing something here. What's so great about golfing?

"You can play by yourself, you don't need a team," my golf addicted colleague tried to explain.

2

"It's a sport you can never master, you're always trying to get better. You meet a lot of people, it's good exercise, and you play in really nice surroundings."

Hmmm, sounds pretty good. Problem is, you can't just tie on a pair of fancy cleats and hit the greens without taking a lesson or two from the pros.

"Amateurs learn to play like amateurs from other amateurs."

Darrell McDonald is head pro at Mill Woods Golf Club. For years he's graciously offered to give me a private lesson. This year I took him up on it.

On a blustery, hot summer day recently, we strolled out to the driving range with a bucket of balls and a couple of borrowed lady's clubs. I hadn't even attempted to hit a ball in years, so I was feeling like a bit of a dolt as Darrell patiently ran me through the basics. Grip, stance, follow through.

"Turn your left foot to 10 o'clock, right foot out to shoulder width. Keep your eye on the ball, and follow through with your swing, with your belly facing the direction of the ball."

I missed a couple, whiffed a couple, and then... swoosh... TING! Oh yeah, the sweet sound of a well-hit golf ball. Even Darrell looked impressed.

"Good eye-hand coordination," he chuckled.

There's something deeply satisfying about getting it right. And there's something deeply aggravating about getting it wrong. Agghh... missed that one. Urrgh... missed it again. Bloody hell. I'm swinging away like a madwoman, my grip so tight I'm developing a blister on my palm. I want to hit it like a man. No, scratch that: I want to hit it like Michelle Wie.

The 16-year-old golf phenom has raised the ire of traditionalists, by insisting on playing with the big boys on the men's tour. Wie's goal is to become the first woman to play in The Masters. A lot of people, most of them men, don't think she belongs there.

And that brings me back to the golf-sex connection.

My "rather-be-celibate-than-go-without-golf" colleague brought in a joke T-shirt the other day that someone had given him for his 40th birthday. On the front was emblazoned the title: 15 REASONS WHY GOLF IS BETTER THAN SEX. Followed by:

#1. It's easier to score in golf.

#2. Golf isn't over in a few minutes.

#3. It's OK to pay for golf.

And my personal favourite?

#13. In golf, women have balls and men don't mind.

I'm rooting for Michelle Wie. I hope she achieves her goal someday, the critics be damned.

As for me? I'm still practising my swing in the bathroom mirror. I figure I need at least two more dates with Darrell before I'm ready to hit the links for real. But I'm starting to understand why golf is such an obsession for so many people. Is it better than sex? That's a question I'm looking forward to answering.

Maybe next summer. ■

3

Tonight's Top Story

(Lynda and her co-anchor and TV spouse Gord Steinke)

My TV Husband

This is a tale of two husbands.

One crawls into bed with me every night, the other shares my makeup.

My "real-life husband" is a handsome police officer named Norm, who helps pay the bills, does most of the yard work, and goes on holidays with me. He's been my best friend for the past 18 years.

My "TV husband" is a handsome journalist named Gord Steinke, who sits beside me nine hours a day, discussing news events, sharing writing tips, and gabbing about life in general. He's also one of my best friends, and we're celebrating our 10th anniversary as co-anchors next week.

That officially makes us the longest-standing news anchor team in Edmonton history.

"You grow old on television, and I'm growing old with you." Gord smiles. "It's sure been fun, and that's why it doesn't seem like 10 years."

I'll admit, it's a confusing relationship sometimes.

Viewers see you together every night in their homes and forget you have a personal life away from the news.

Even my young nephew was befuddled years ago. When he heard my husband and I were coming for dinner, he expected to see Gord. When reminded that "Auntie Lynda is married to Uncle Norm", my nephew looked horrified and whispered, "Does Gord know?"

The public is often confused too.

"When you're out shopping, people think 'Well there's Gord — Lynda can't be far behind." My co-anchor laughs. "They just expect that when I'm out buying a loaf of bread, that you'll be around the corner buying tomatoes. So they're kinda shocked when they see you out with your real spouse."

Gord's long-suffering wife Deb handles the confusion by graciously extending her hand and saying, "Hi, I'm the other Lynda".

Our anchor colleagues can relate.

Global Morning Edition anchor Shaye Ganam says he's "been an item" with his co-host Andrea Engel for eight years now.

"I spend more waking hours with her than my wife! Thank God we get along. Believe it or not, there's never been one single fight."

Citytv anchor Paul Mennier says he "works hard on the chemistry" with co-anchor Jennifer Martin. "Nagging, bitching, correcting... praising, encouraging and listening. Kinda like a marriage."

CTV's Daryl McIntyre has been to the anchor altar several times in the past 17 years. "I'm on my fourth 'marriage'. Daphne, Leslie, Shawna and now Carrie."

The co-anchor relationship is unique. The boss puts a couple of strangers together in a high stress environment and hopes for chemistry — and not the explosive kind either.

Sometimes it works - sometimes it doesn't.

Gord was once teamed up with a female anchor in the States who threw her head back each night seconds before air time and insisted he look up her nose to check for... shall we say... foreign matter. The last time I saw her, she was anchoring on CNN.

There's no booger patrol on the Global anchor desk, but Gord is quite comfortable letting me know if I have a hair growing out of my chin. I return the favour by yanking out his two-inch eyebrow hairs.

"It seems like every night there's a big gut-wrenching laugh." Gord chuckles. "Every night is fun, isn't it? And I think people pick up on that. They know we're having fun."

But this is the news after all, and we've also shared a lot of unhappiness. The deadly Pine Lake tornado. 9/11. The Whyte Avenue fire. The tsunami. Bus crashes, floods, gang murders, and the list goes on.

We've done at least ten elections together, sitting side-by-side watching the results come in, excited as anyone else to see who's going to be the next mayor or prime minister.

We rang in the new millennium from the anchor desk, wore touques and mitts to broadcast from the Heritage Classic in minus 30 weather, donned football jerseys for a newscast from City Hall when the Eskies were in the Grey Cup.

"It's like working with your best friend," Gord smiles. "The chemistry clicked right off the bat, and it's been a blast. That's why it doesn't seem like 10 years."

Happy anniversary, my friend and TV husband. Here's to many more. ■

(Lynda reporting live from the Alberta Legislature during centennial celebrations in 2005)

News Ageism

I have a confession to make: I'm not 25 anymore. I'm not even 35, and that's a dangerous admission for any professional woman to make.

Many of my fortysomething girlfriends are straining against the proverbial glass ceiling, watching younger, less experienced people slide into plum positions they've worked so hard and so long to attain. It's equally galling when a man with exactly the same qualifications gets the gold-plated key to the executive washroom by virtue of gender.

Turning 40 is like drinking some mad scientist's potion; slowly but surely you turn invisible, without benefit of any comic book super powers.

This ageism is rampant in many professions, but if you think your industry is bad, try working in television news. It's not only age fixated, it's sexist too.

I'm a female news anchor who has spent 20 years in the business. I've covered dozens of elections, tagged along on late night police raids, even watched brain surgery from the operating room. I like to think my experience and maturity make me a better journalist.

So why is it that when a male anchor ages on air, his receding hairline, wrinkles and love handles conjure up words like wisdom, respect, trust and credibility? Yet when a female anchor gets older, she's considered to be matronly, soft, over the hill and on her way out?

We all love Lloyd Robertson. He's a Canadian institution, a broadcasting legend, a man to be admired. But what if Lloyd had a twin sister named Louise? Picture it: Lloyd with slightly longer hair, red lipstick, mascara, perhaps a string of pearls. Is that the face of a million-dollar network news anchor? I think not.

God bless Barbara Walters. In 1976, she became the first woman in North America to co-anchor a nightly network newscast.

She was teamed with the curmudgeonly Harry Reasoner, ABC's superstar newscaster of the era.

Sadly, Barbara had barely warmed up the seat before she was punted from the anchor desk. Turns out Harry wasn't wild about a co-anchor, let alone a female co-anchor.

Fast forward two decades, and pretty much the same thing happened north of the border to the pride of Wadena, Saskatchewan, Pamela Wallin.

In 1992, Wallin became the first woman in Canada to co-anchor a national prime time newscast when she was teamed with the CBC's Peter Mansbridge.

Less than three years later, Wallin was unceremoniously dumped when CBC executives felt the Peter/Pam experiment was a failure.

Don't get me wrong, there are mature female television news stars out there. We have CBC's Alison Smith, Global's Deirdre McMurdy and CTV's Sandi Rinaldo.

In the States, think Diane Sawyer, Paula Zahn, Katie Couric, Connie Chung or Lesley Stahl.

They're all over the age of 45, some well over. These are extremely talented newswomen, but every one of them is relegated to the land of late night, morning or weekend television.

CNN and Fox employ a lot of women, many in high-profile positions, but the truth is, mainstream network news is still where it's at in my industry. That's where the viewers are, that's where the money and respect are.

There are only six coveted network anchor positions in all of North America — CBS, NBC and ABC in the U.S.; Global, CTV and CBC in Canada. In every case, those big-ticket jobs are filled by men.

You wouldn't pick a surgeon based on looks or gender. You'd want the most skilled person for the job. So why would only middle-aged men be capable of delivering a national prime-time newscast? Oh sure, there are lots of female anchors in local television news, but they're too often perky blonds straight out of journalism school, paired up with older, greying male co-anchors.

To be fair, this is a much bigger problem south of the border. Here at home, my company, Global Television, has proven itself to be an equal-opportunity employer. Six on-air personalities in my newsroom are women perched on the edge of 40 or over. I feel good about that. I wish it was the industry standard, but sadly it is not.

This ageist fixation in the mass media has made women like me fearful of revealing our true age. Will we scuttle future job opportunities? I was once told by an American TV agent that at 35, I was "too old" to get a job in the States. What a load of hooey.

Another talented journalist I know was advised to erase all the dates on her resume so potential employers would actually look at her resume tape, instead of seeing her age and throwing her application in the garbage. That's just wrong whether you work in TV, the airline industry, the classroom or a corporate boardroom. It doesn't matter what you do for a living — women need to help change these ageist attitudes that hurt other women and prevent them from reaching their true potential.

That change starts with confidently embracing our age, being proud of who we are, where we've been and the lessons we've learned along the way.

So here goes. It's confession time. I'm 43, and feeling darn good about it. ■

3

Katie Makes History

"Oh for God's sake. It's that bloody woman from Edmonton again, requesting an interview. Why doesn't she just drop it?"

Well, you can't blame a gal for trying.

Katie Couric is one of my broadcasting heroes. First of all she's smart. She's a tough, but compassionate interviewer who does her homework, a journalist who's not afraid to act silly on occasion. She laughs, she cries, she's real.

I actually met Katie in New York a few summers ago. I walked right up to her and stared her intently in the eye. She didn't even blink. OK, it was Madame Tussaud's, but I was fascinated. I'm five foot seven and Katie was looking into my chin. She's a little slip of a thing with a charming crooked smile and the tiniest teeth you'll ever see.

When I heard she was being considered for the CBS Evening News chair I was hopeful. When I heard she'd accepted the job I was delighted.

Exactly two years ago I wrote my first column for the Edmonton Journal, about why there were no women in high-powered network anchor jobs on either side of the border.

I bemoaned the fact that while women had made great strides in television news, the industry was still largely age fixated and sexist. Why did the plum anchor jobs have to always go to men? Why did network executives think only middle-aged white male anchors were capable of delivering a prime-time newscast?

So when CBS had the guts to break with tradition and hire a woman for the coveted Evening News anchor job, I was surprised, and heartened.

Katie Couric is making history. The next edition of Trivial Pursuit will ask under the category green for television, "Who was the first woman to be named solo anchor of a nightly network newscast?"

I have so many questions for Katie. How is she handling the pressure of being the first female network anchor? What does a woman bring to the anchor desk that a man may not? What's the reaction been like so far? But two voice-mails and one pleading email to her personal assistant have gone unanswered.

3

In interviews south of the border she's downplayed the female factor, saying gender is not an issue when it comes to her new high-powered anchor job. She does admit though, that even her 10-year-old daughter insisted she take the position saying "Mom you've got to do this. You're the first woman to do this job by yourself." The reported $15 million a year salary doesn't hurt either.

Katie Couric's debut broadcast was on Sept. 5th. The ratings that night blew the roof off at CBS headquarters in New York. They were 86 per cent higher than the average news audience a year ago.

Even legendary newsman Walter Cronkite has been quoted as saying, "I think she's doing a great job."

So Katie has finally, and so far successfully, broken the glass ceiling in the male-dominated world of network news anchors, but can she save CBS?

There's a disturbing trend afoot in network and local television news. The audience is disappearing. A survey by the Pew Research Center for the People and the Press done last July uncovered some disheartening statistics. The number of people who regularly watch nightly network news has plummeted from 60 per cent in 1993, to just 28 per cent in 2006. That's not good news.

Are there too many choices available? Are more people turning to the Internet to get their news fix? Is the audience becoming cynical about the way television news is being presented? All interesting questions and fodder for a future column.

In the meantime, I'd still love to talk to Katie Couric. Maybe I'll give it another try next fall when she's celebrated her first full year in the anchor chair. She might not be as busy then.

Or we could always have another rendezvous at Madame Tussaud's. ■

(photo courtesy, John Lucas, Edmonton Journal)

Looking For A Little Good News

Have you ever turned off a television newscast, or bypassed the morning paper because you thought it was just too bloody negative? Or just too bloody for that matter?

Well I can't say as I blame you. Some days even veteran journalists shake their heads about the unnecessary suffering in the world, the senseless crimes, the devastating natural disasters, the manifestation of pure evil on earth.

It used to be that once every 10 years or so, you'd witness a piece of video that made the hair stand up on the back of your neck. A story so mind-blowing, you'd always remember exactly where you were when you first saw or heard about it.

We're not getting those blessed 10-year intervals anymore. Now the madness seems to come at us pretty much monthly, and the scale of the atrocities is increasing. The Pickton murder trial. The Columbine school massacre. The

9/11 terrorist attacks on America. Teenagers beaten or stabbed to death at parties.

The trick is not to be numbed by it. As a journalist, you have to really "feel" every new horror that surfaces so you don't lose your humanity in the process.

So it's worth re-examining that old media saw "if it bleeds, it leads," the implication being that journalists are one part human, two parts vampire, salivating at the idea of a new juicy horror to exploit over the supper hour, or on the front page of the daily paper.

For example, some people say the media shouldn't cover school shootings, that it only encourages copycat attacks. But I suggest to you, if a madman took a high-powered rifle into an Edmonton high school and began slaughtering students and staff and the media ignored it, we'd face the immediate wrath of family members and friends desperate for information.

We try to cover stories that are of the greatest interest, or informational value to the public. If everyone's talking about snow removal for example — we focus on that. If a trend toward teen violence appears to be emerging — we focus on that, talking to experts to see what's happening, and how can we fix it.

We are not opposed to delivering good news, far from it. In fact, some journalists and news organizations are deliberately moving away from the "dark side."

Former CNN anchor Daryn Kagan quit her lucrative day job last September, to launch a strictly "good news" website, www.darynkagan.com.

The former TV anchor explained to her fans that, "It's important to be informed, but I also think it's important to be inspired."

A quick scan of Kagan's site revealed daily stories like a former prostate cancer patient who quit the corporate world to lead life-altering nature trips, or the professional chef who whips up gourmet meals for the homeless at a New York soup kitchen.

Then there's www.happynews.com, where the credo is "real news, compelling stories, always positive."

The website was set up last year in response to a belief that the mainstream media reports too much negative news. The criteria are simple. Stories must be happy or positive, and 100-per-cent accurate. Not a bad idea, but consider this:

The Radio-Television News Directors Foundation in Washington, D.C. released its "Future of News Survey" in 2006. Despite the emerging new media, 65.5 per cent of people surveyed named local television news as one of their top three sources for news. 28.4 per cent named local newspapers, and 28.3 per cent named national network television news. Only 11.2 per cent surveyed named the Internet.

So you're sticking with local news, and I thank you for that. Now let's work together to build a better newscast and a better newspaper. What do you like, what turns you off? Give your favourite media outlet some constructive criticism, or even kudos if you like.

The bad news stories have a way of presenting themselves. We need to hear about the positive stories in your community. So don't be afraid to pick up the phone and spread the good news.

Together, maybe we can help portray a more positive Edmonton in the future. ■

3

From Paris To Anna Nicole - Defining Real News

If I see one more story about Paris Hilton, I'm going to drive an ice pick into my forehead.

She's a spoiled, rich, party girl who's famous for being famous — a blond clothes horse who would show up at the opening of a door if it meant free champagne and paparazzi.

Why are the media obsessed with the hotel heiress saga? Is Joe Average really sitting on the edge of his recliner breathlessly waiting for the latest Paris-goes-to-jail update?

Is this really news?

According to the self-proclaimed Voice of Authority, Merriam-Webster's Collegiate Dictionary, the definition of news is:

1a) a report of recent events

1b) previously unknown information

2a) material reported in a newspaper or news periodical or on a newscast

2b) matter that is newsworthy.

OK, what's the definition of newsworthy?

"Sufficiently interesting to the general public to warrant reporting."

But who decides what's "sufficiently interesting"? We the media do, and it's becoming a tricky business, as newsrooms try to strike a precarious and often controversial balance between news you need to know, and infotainment.

The lines are being blurred on big network news shows like CNN's Anderson Cooper 360 Degrees.

One day the focus is on the U.S. presidential race, the next it's all about analyzing Anna Nicole's final autopsy report.

The day she died, a breaking-news alert flashed at the top of computer screens throughout the newsroom.

"Hey — Anna Nicole Smith is dead!" Colleagues shouted.

"What? You're kidding! Where did you hear that?"

"It's on the wires. Do we have time to change the opener?"

It was surprising news.

For weeks, Smith had been making headlines for her sordid he-said/she-said paternity dispute, and the tragic death of her adult son. It was a final sad chapter in the complicated and somewhat pathetic life of another celebrity who was famous for being infamous. I felt sorry for Anna Nicole.

But was her death newsworthy? Yes, gauging by the reaction of colleagues and friends, it seemed to fit Webster's criteria of "sufficiently interesting." Was it newsworthy enough to merit front-page headlines and wall-to-wall television coverage?

By Day 5 of "all-Anna-all-the-time," I was ready to scream. Part of me thought this woman who desperately craved celebrity would be delighted to know that in death, she was finally important enough to usurp the national news agenda in the States, and even here in Canada to a lesser degree. Part of me thought the media had been sucked into a curious and disturbing tabloid feeding frenzy.

We had spirited debates around the newsroom meeting table. Some colleagues thought the Anna Nicole story had legs and was a source of great interest to our viewers. Some of us thought enough was enough; it was time to move on. If the viewers were dying to know the minutiae of a seriously mixed-up life, they could make a date with Nancy Grace or Larry King Live.

The "sufficiently interesting, but is it really news?" debate resurfaced recently with the release of a disturbing voice mail from a famous and furious father.

Alec Baldwin, clearly enraged, was caught on tape ranting at his 11-year-old estranged daughter, Ireland.

Across the newsroom, colleagues paused to listen to the Baldwin tirade. In the editorial meeting that afternoon, we argued over whether it had a place in the 6 p.m. newscast.

"People are talking about it — they'll want to see it at 6." a producer argued.

"But it's not news, it's an actor losing it on his daughter — who cares?" a colleague challenged.

In the end, we compromised, cutting the original two-minute story down to about 30 seconds.

It's the proverbial chicken-and-egg debate.

Are the media force-feeding readers and viewers an unhealthy fast-food diet of infotainment — news tidbits that appear to be tasty but have no real substance and leave you hungry for more?

Or are the media simply responding to society's growing obsession with celebrity, and diminishing attention span for global issues like the genocide in Darfur?

I leave it to you to decide. ■

In the Eye of the News Storm

July 31, 1987.

It started off as a sleepy day in the ITV newsroom with a skeleton crew and no bosses in-house.

We were heading into a long weekend, and the six o'clock newscast was preempted by a live football game. Without the usual deadlines, the late afternoon vibe in the newsroom was unusually relaxed. Reporters were filing their stories early, and waving as they headed out the door, looking forward to a little extra R & R over the August Civic Holiday long weekend.

I was a rookie reporter who was asked to cover off the assignment desk that day. My job was nearly done, when the sky began turning an ominous shade of khaki green. We were clearly in for one heck of a thunderstorm.

The hail began falling around four that afternoon, huge stones - some as big as softballs.

Our senior cameraman Hank Imes was one of the few staffers still around, so I sent him out to get shots of the hail for our 10 o'clock newscast. Little did we know we were about to find ourselves in the eye of a massive news storm.

The assignment desk phone began ringing with calls from worried viewers.

"Hey, have you guys heard about the hail in south Edmonton? It actually shattered my windshield!"

The calls began ramping up in intensity.

"You guys better get a camera out here right now – a car is flipped over and people are trapped inside."

Then this:

"You won't believe it, but a train has been blown right off the tracks in South Edmonton!"

By now, every light is flashing on the assignment desk phone. Something bizarre is going on out there, and I have no staff to send out to investigate.

This was an era of no cell phones - no computers – no live trucks or news helicopters - no weather radio alarms, or emergency broadcast systems. The ITV cameramen had simple CB radios in their cars.

"CJZ-304 – this is the assignment desk calling Unit three. Can you hear me? (static) CJZ-304 the desk is calling Unit four - can you hear me? (static) Can ANYONE out there hear me?"

My senior cameraman Hank was in the bowels of the building using a blow dryer to clear his waterlogged viewfinder. We were desperate, so the camera was slapped back together, and Hank hit the highway bound for Sherwood Park. Traffic was going nowhere, so he tucked in behind a fire truck, plunged through a water filled ditch, and then headed down the wrong side of the freeway toward the biggest shock of his life.

"I looked around and saw a swath of destruction cut in a line north and south of the freeway," Hank recalls.

"Buildings, vehicles, trees, power lines, everything tumbled and wrecked."

An F4 tornado travelling 416 kilometres an hour had touched down in Leduc. The twister was on the ground for a full hour destroying everything in it's path for 40 kilometres. 27 people were dead, hundreds more injured, and 300 homes had been obliterated.

The ITV newsroom was now in full scramble mode – reporters, cameramen and editors were rushing back to work, and together we assembled a special breaking news broadcast to air at 5:30 that afternoon.

The raw video was literally quite shocking, and I joined Doug Main on the anchor desk to watch it live and unedited with our fellow Edmontonians - the first time viewers had seen or heard of the devastation.

On the biggest weather day in Edmonton's history, ITV's beloved forecaster Bill Matheson was trapped at home by flooding in his neighbourhood, so the job of explaining the weather disaster to viewers fell to a young reporter named Neill Fitzpatrick, now Global's News Director.

"I was terrified to be honest." Neill admits.

"I had no idea what had just happened, only sketchy reports of the extent of the damage, and I had absolutely no idea what caused any tornado."

Neill was coached over the phone by Bill, who carefully explained how the weather ingredients had combined to create the perfect storm, so to speak.

By suppertime, the entire news team was in place, long weekend plans abandoned, and we dug in for a heartbreaking and exhausting four days of wall to wall coverage.

When I finally left the newsroom early the next morning, I was startled to hear laughter and music coming from the bar next door to the station. I felt like running inside and screaming "Don't you people know what just happened? 27 people are DEAD!"

July 31st, 1987.

Black Friday transformed me from a naïve cub reporter, into a grizzled news veteran in a matter of hours. It was, without question, the worst day of my career. ■

3

Estrogen On The Airwaves

Quick — name three marquee female radio hosts in Canada — bonus points if you can name one female radio star in Edmonton in the highly coveted morning time slot. You have 30 seconds — go!

Time's running out… having trouble? Let's make this a little easier. Name TWO famous, highly paid Canadian female radio hosts currently on the air. 15 seconds… 10… five… Sorry, time's up.

Not so easy is it? We've come a long way baby, from the days of fedora-sporting media men with press cards tucked into the brims of their hats. The Journal newsroom is now full of talented female writers and editors. The vast majority of students interested in television news are women, to the point where local TV newsrooms are often desperate to hire qualified men to even out the balance. So why are the top radio jobs in this country still filled almost exclusively by men?

Oh sure, women can find work in radio, if they're satisfied doing traffic reports, reading the news, playing the sex- pot, or second banana to the highly paid male morning show jock. Very few have their own shows in prime time, and very few make the six-figure salary of their male counterparts.

I took a quick spin across the Edmonton radio dial, and when it comes to the highly coveted morning host slot, there's a whole lot of testosterone on the airwaves. Check this out:

CHED Radio — male host

CISN — two male hosts, 1 female host

Joe FM — two male hosts

K-Rock — three male hosts

Magic 99 — male host

The Bounce – 2 male hosts

CBC Edmonton AM — male host

Sonic FM — male host

3

The Bear — primary host male (co-hosts one male, one female)

A veteran male deejay in town privately confessed, "I've been thinking about it, and you're right. It IS an old boy's club, and there's no reason for it."

To be fair, women have managed to secure a handful of morning show slots in Edmonton. EZ Rock has a male/female morning team, so does CFCW and the Big Earl. The person who does the hiring for those last two country stations is a woman. Coincidence?

"I was looking for the best 'man' for the job… and they just happened to be ladies," says Jackie Rae Greening, a successful radio host herself.

Most people I know don't really care if the host is a man or a woman, as long as they're interesting, articulate, intelligent and amusing. So why the dramatic gender imbalance?

Kristina Perkins is a radio instructor at NAIT. She says private market research done for stations over the years has allegedly uncovered strong listener preferences for male hosts, but warns, "I can almost guarantee none of them will want to share this data."

Popular K-Rock midday host Melissa Wright admits there does seem to be a preference for "guy talk" on the radio — fart jokes and football scores — but she partially blames what she calls women's "biological bitchiness" for the gender inequities in radio, a competitiveness not seen in men.

"Men think funny men are funny," Melissa explains.

"Women hear a funny woman (or God forbid a sexy-sounding woman), and they generally see them as competition and want to scratch their eyes out."

Marty Forbes is general manager of the Standard Radio group in Edmonton, a self-professed "huge fan of female broadcasters," who points out that two of his stations have women on their morning shows.

"Only negative that we end up with, is the fact that women often 'leave' the industry for long periods of time (maternity leaves)… men stay in for the long haul."

Forbes says it's important to note that he has several female managers behind the scenes, which is "just as important."

Maybe more women in radio management will mean more women behind the microphone in key roles. That, plus an increase in the number of women applying for the NAIT radio program in recent years, and new opportunities being offered up by satellite radio, and maybe — just maybe — women will finally be able to kick down the door to that old boy's radio club.

You go girls...we're listening. ■

3

The Global News Team - Gord Steinke, Lynda and Sports Anchor John Sexsmith

TV Bloopers

Some people think television news anchors are egomaniacal, overpaid nitwits who walk around in a cloud of hairspray.

The profession's been getting a bum rap ever since WJM anchorman Ted Baxter bumbled his way onto the small screen on Mary Tyler Moore.

Tinseltown may love to lampoon the TV anchor, but in real life — when the red light goes on and you're live — you'd better have your wits about you. Consider these real-life TV moments:

PANHANDLER PANIC

I'm standing outside the courthouse. It's 30 seconds to air. A young panhandler approaches looking for change. I make the mistake of telling him we're seconds away from going live — so he leans up against me and says "I won't leave unless you give me a loonie!"

My cameraman madly checks his pockets for coins as the producer yells in my earpiece "Who's that guy? Get rid of that guy!"

We're now 10 seconds to air. In desperation I tell the panhandler "The reporter from CFRN has a loonie!" So he toodles off in her direction to fudge up the competition's live hit. (Hey, it's live TV... you do what you gotta do.)

COLLAPSING KIDDIE CASTLE

Former Global meteorologist Claire Martin decides to do weather live from inside an inflatable tent full of children at the Taste of Edmonton festival. Unfortunately the cameraman has plugged the live truck into an outlet that is draining power to the Kiddie Castle.

Claire says, "As I got closer to the live hit, I could feel the walls around me start to sag."

She kicks off the live weathercast by taking a dramatic leap. "As I landed on the softening base of the castle, I launched every child inside into the air, traumatizing them instantly," Claire recalls.

(The kids cried. The weather hit was wrapped up early.)

INNER-CITY ATTACK

Former ITV show Rockincountry goes on location with host Mike Sobel playing a comedic character interviewing up-and-coming musical artists.

Sobel is sitting on the fire escape of a condemned building downtown dressed as a drunk homeless person when Mike says, "An actual inebriated homeless person approached me with a broken bottle in his hand threatening to take me out because he thought I was making fun of him.

"I assumed the crew would come to my rescue, but instead they kept rolling tape hoping to capture real drama.

"We were doing reality programming long before its time!"

GOOD GOURD

A proud contestant in the Smoky Lake great pumpkin competition hauls her giant gourd into the CFRN studios for a live interview.

Anchor Joel Gotlib decides to make the live hit more active, thinking "Why not show the viewers at home how heavy these pumpkins are?"

He says "As I pulled on the stem I heard a cracking sound... the stem snapped off and I fell back a few steps."

Horrified, he asks the pumpkin's owner "What criteria do the judge's base their decision on?" Turns out the 200-pound prize gourd is automatically disqualified.

Gotlib says "The incident earned me the nickname Pumpkin Killer."

SPIDER CO-HOST

Global Troubleshooter Julie Matthews was anchoring the late news in Lloydminster years ago when, "Out of the corner of my eye I saw a huge black spider slowly lowering from the ceiling on its string of web... It was difficult to maintain a straight, relaxed face and continue reading the news.

"The spider came closer and closer until I was sure viewers would be able to see it twirling not far from my face.

"As soon as we hit the next story... I grabbed my script and ended the spider's television debut. I still laugh about it!"

BAD TIMING

Former ITV Troubleshooter Sandra Blaikie was reporting in Sudbury, Ontario, when her station's distinguished 6 o'clock anchor was caught on tape in a compromising position.

His microphone was cutting out, so Sandra says, "He rolls his chair back a little from the anchor desk and the cameraman gets down on his hands and knees between the anchor's legs to jiggle the connection.

"Time's running out fast, and the cameraman doesn't seem to get it. He keeps fiddling while the countdown comes... 3... 2... 1... and we're back live with the anchor looking horrified and a cameraman's back visible to the viewers between his knees.

"Oh my God it was the funniest thing I ever saw."

TV news. It's live, it's unpredictable, it's responsible for many horrifying and hilarious moments.

So c'mon. Give us a break folks... ■

3

The Big Picture

Childless By Choice

When I was in Grade two I nearly killed my brother.

We were crouched on top of an old dresser in the basement throwing paper airplanes. Mine was flying farther, so my brother leapt off the dresser, ran to the corner and crumpled my plane, then scrambled back up to throw his again. I did the only sensible thing I could… pushed him off the dresser.

Brad konked his head on the concrete floor with enough force to cause a seemingly unstoppable nosebleed. I felt quite justified in my actions, and was rather annoyed to learn I had a date with the wooden spoon once the crisis was over.

As my parents fussed over my bleeding brother, I pulled on my snow pants in a huff and decided to run away. THAT would show them. I marched to the end of the block and sat in a snow bank waiting for the missing child dragnet to arrive.

An hour later, I gave up and trudged home with a frozen bum, and a head full of steam.

Ah, never a dull moment in the Steele household. Poor Mom.

I imagine that having children is both the greatest blessing and biggest challenge in life. I say imagine, because despite the fact I intended to have at least one of my own, it just never happened.

I could blame shift work, or career aspirations, but the truth is my maternal clock has never had batteries, and apparently I have some company in this regard.

According to a 2001 survey by Statistics Canada nearly one in 10 Canadians does not plan to have children. The reasons range from "Not having met the right partner, living with a partner who does not want children, or having a career that is too fulfilling or demanding to allow time for the care of a child."

In a 2003 report called Childfree by Choice Statscan researchers wrote: "Those who opt to stay childfree constitute a small minority that often feel obliged to justify their decision… It appears our 'kidcentric' society tends to leave those without children feeling inadequate, left out, judged or misunderstood."

4

I don't feel inadequate. Misunderstood maybe. My decision not to have children doesn't mean I don't love "other" people's children.

Whenever a day-glow fur pumpkin waddles up my front porch and hollers "HALLOWEEN APPLES!" I turn into the warm and fuzzy Grinch at the end of the movie, all sappy smiles, with a cartoon heart pulsing with love for a knee-high human being I've never met.

I would donate an organ to my niece or nephews. Take a bullet in their stead.

They are beautiful and special young people. I'm proud of them, and would do anything for them. I just don't need children of my own.

Some people don't get it, saying "Who's going to take care of you when you're old and frail?"

Well — in a perfect world I'll grow old with my best friend, my husband. But if fate determines I'm the last one standing, I have a plan.

I'll gather up some of my girlfriends and we'll rent a house on a cliff in Greece. We'll sit on the porch, sip chilled white wine, play cards, and get fat, as we watch the sun dip into the sea each night.

Family. It's a word with many definitions. ■

Rude Kids

Is it just me, or are children becoming more disrespectful?

When I was a kid, you wouldn't dare be rude to a grown-up. Didn't matter if you knew them or not. You simply did not treat an adult with anything less than respect.

Growing up in the '60s, my friends and I always said "yes please", and "thank you very much." We were expected to write thank-you letters for gifts. We called our parents' friends by their formal surnames.

Were we born nice kids? Nah. Good manners were ingrained at a very early age. If you slipped up you got your butt paddled with the wooden spoon.

So what's going on with today's generation of youngsters?

Don't get me wrong — 98 per cent of young people I meet these days are pleasant, friendly and respectful. It's the other two per cent that have me worried.

Read-in Week is always an interesting experience. Most of the kids are excited to have a stranger in their midst telling stories. It's a nice break in the routine, and if the guest is someone their folks might watch on TV occasionally, well, even better as far as they're concerned. But in recent years, it seems there's always at least one kid in the bunch who's determined to hijack the experience with rudeness.

One memorable eight-year-old snapped at me to "Just hurry up and read the book!" That was followed up by "Didn't you bring any souvenirs from Global? You should give us all a loonie then."

I looked around for the teacher, expecting her to give the kid's ear a twist and haul him off to the principal's office. But no… she didn't seem to even notice.

Maybe she wanted a mental break from her students. Maybe she was used to this kid's disrespectful behaviour. Or maybe she knew there was really nothing she could do, because even though this boy needed a royal kick in the rear, I suppose you're not allowed to manhandle the children anymore, lest their parents file some sort of complaint with the school board.

A colleague of mine was in an Edmonton junior high school recently doing a story about a popular teen website called Nexopia. City police were concerned naive users could be sexually exploited.

4

As the news crew was taking shots of the website, a group of teenage girls angry about the negative publicity aimed at their favorite chat site, began taunting the female reporter. They called her "ugly and stupid" and asked if she wanted to have a fistfight. Disgraceful.

If these "bad seed" kids aren't overtly rude, they're often dismissive.

I waited patiently at a store counter the other day while the teenage clerk flirted with her male co-worker. When she finally got around to serving me, her bubbly demeanor switched to sullen, as though I was deliberately making her life difficult by trying to actually buy something.

Someone needs to explain the concept of customer service to this generation.

I got my first job as a waitress at the age of 13. If I had treated the customers like a pain in the a** I would have been fired on the spot.

But here's the thing that really concerns me. What about that small percentage of teens who show their disrespect for others by committing crimes against their own neighbours?

My house was broken into a few years back. The thieves made off with several Christmas presents including a brand new CD player still inside the box. My police officer husband used to work in the forensic identification section, so he dusted the point of entry himself, and found a partial fingerprint. It belonged to a teenager. They never caught the culprit, but the crime left me seething. Where were this kid's parents? How come they didn't wonder where Johnny suddenly got all the cash from?

I bet it wasn't the first time this young offender had smashed in someone's window. You get away with it, you do it again… and again and again and again… until you're caught.

They say it takes an entire village to raise a child.

I guess that makes us all responsible for the behaviour of the next generation. If that's the case, I think we're not collectively doing enough to instill the importance of respect for one another.

Bad behaviour with no consequences begets more bad behaviour, and that's a serious problem.

Because rude and disrespectful children grow up to be rude and disrespectful adults. ■

4

A Sea of Blue Polyester

I'm amazed by how elegant today's high school grads look, with their strapless gowns and tuxedos, the whole gang piling into a limousine for a twilight tour of the city before the big grad night shindig.

They look like young Hollywood stars. Tousled up-dos for the girls, and just the right amount of facial hair and swagger for the guys. You look at these bright, shiny young people and just for a minute you forget they're really teenagers disguised as sophisticated adults.

I looked more like Klondike Kate than Kate Hudson on my high school graduation day in Hinton.

Powder blue was big in 1978. My gown was a floor length confection of ruffles and elasticized puffy sleeves with a Victorian style high collar made of lace. My hair was a small town version of the Farrah Fawcett, with bangs and fringe hot ironed into sausage rolls of hair.

My graduation photo needed to be retouched, because two weeks before the big day, I felt a pimple coming on, and fried my skin by desperately pressing wedges of toilet paper soaked in aftershave to the offending spot, until my skin was raw and cracked. Not a pretty picture.

There was no fancy gala evening like the kids have today, no four-course dinner with family. My grad ceremony took place in a musty high school gymnasium gussied up with balloons and twirls of crepe paper.

We were assigned a grand march partner from our graduation class based on height. You were supposed to file into the gym to the cheers of family and friends, then do a waltz with the lights dimmed low.

But there weren't enough guys in the class of '78. So my grand march partners were named Steve and Holly. We joked about doing a butterfly at the end, but instead did the first dance with our folks. It was a preview of my wedding night waltz, smiling awkwardly and stepping on Dad's toes.

With the formalities behind us, it was time for the real party to begin. The Klondike Kate attire was replaced by jeans, and a convoy of vehicles headed for the predetermined bush party.

Today's grads are a lot smarter than we were. They get someone else to drive.

4

I grew up in an era that incredibly, and stupidly, wasn't worried about drinking and driving. We were more concerned about getting a ticket for having open liquor in the vehicle than we were about getting an impaired. A few friends of mine paid the price for that ignorance with their lives.

We were young and we were naive. We did not have the pressures that today's teens face.

To be truthful, I was not a great student in those days. My focus was on socializing. It was all about the friends and the boyfriends. If I was graduating today with that attitude and those marks, I'd have virtually no chance of being accepted to university.

Maybe that's why today's high school grads look so much older than they really are.

Society is pressuring them at a very early age to plan for the future.

Instead of enjoying the naive bliss of childhood as long as possible, many are anxious to find careers that will make them rich quick — or dreaming of instant fame enjoyed by their peers on reality shows like American Idol.

And that pressure seems to block some teens from moving forward. They're staying at home longer, not venturing out on their own, claiming it's cheaper and more comfortable to live with Mom and Dad.

Maybe they're staying at home, because they really just want to be kids for a little while longer before they face the harsh reality of life on their own. You know… responsibility, bills, bosses.

I think it's tough to be a teenager in 2006.

I'm glad I grew up in the '70's. There was less pressure, more fun, and in the end I think my generation turned out just fine.

Life is tough enough. Here's to letting kids be kids. ■

4

The Trouble With Teens

When I graduated from high school in 1978, people settled their disagreements with words, rarely fists. Pot was the drug of choice, Pong was the hot video game on the market, and we watched benign sitcoms on TV like Fish, and WKRP in Cincinnati.

I didn't know anyone who carried a weapon to school. No one was murdered and no classmate of mine ever went to jail for assaulting another human being. We were afraid of the police, even more afraid of disappointing our parents. If we screwed up, there were consequences. We knew the rules, and for the most part we respected them.

So when did it become OK to beat homeless people to death? To take baseball bats to house parties or bully classmates into committing suicide? It's sickening.

I don't understand the changing values, but I have some theories.

First of all, teens today are growing up in a faster paced, high tech and often dangerous world, where the six o'clock news is a never-ending horror reel of terrorist attacks, Mountie massacres and random school shootings.

Children play virtual reality video games that reward players for blowing off the heads of police officers or murdering prostitutes.

Drugs in my day were pretty much limited to low-grade marijuana, and hash. Today's drug dealers are peddling cheap chemical highs made of toxic ingredients that destroy brain cells, and turn teens into instant addicts.

When I went to high school, divorce was not an issue. Ninety-nine per cent of the kids lived in a home with two parents. Today's classrooms are filled with children from broken homes, and children who live in homes where both parents are working. Are teens today not getting enough quality time with their most important role models? Is that contributing to an increase in teen violence? I honestly don't know.

The gap between the haves and have-nots is widening. We were fashion conscious in the '70s, but we weren't asking our parents for $200 to buy designer jeans, or text-messaging friends on our personal cell phones during math class.

In this booming Alberta economy, poverty is still a big issue for many families who can't afford to give their kids the luxuries so many other young people enjoy.

4

These have-not teens often feel ostracized and unfairly penalized. I can see why some may be tempted to cross the line to get what they feel they deserve to fit in.

I spent a morning recently with some Grade 12 students from the Edmonton area. I wanted to know what they thought was fueling teen violence. They talked about how easy it was to get weapons.

"You can go to Wal-Mart and buy a knife," said one young man.

They talked about the media, and the level of violence they see on a regular basis. There was a lack of respect for the justice system.

"I think our courts are a joke, you know."

One teen said he knew a guy who attacked and paralyzed another young man.

"All he gets is two years in jail. The other guy's life is ruined forever."

Were they not afraid of the consequences then?

"It's not that there are no consequences," a teenage boy explained. "It's just that once you're angry, you stop thinking about what you're doing, and you just do it."

Well my generation got angry too, but we didn't stab people to death at parties, so what gives?

"It's cool nowadays to have a rep as being some crazy kind of guy who beats people up," a male student admitted.

So is the real problem a lack of compassion and empathy? One earnest young man agreed.

"If everyone cared about everyone else, there wouldn't be any youth violence at all."

It's clearly a big and complex problem, too big for just one column. So what's the solution?

I've been talking to some local criminologists and educators who have interesting thoughts on the subject. Stay tuned for more on that.

In the meantime, if you've got any clever ideas, drop me an e-mail. We're all affected by teen violence, and we're all going to have to be part of the solution. ■

The Search For Solutions

"Good kids come from good families."

Those are the simple, yet profound words of an Edmonton teacher who's spent 43 years in the public school system. Janet has observed many societal changes since the early 1960s, like a dramatic rise in the number of single parent families. The veteran educator says many parents today don't have the energy to feed their children properly, read to them, mentor them, or help them do their homework. The result? Angry little children in classrooms, who sometimes grow up to be angry adults.

Janet is one of dozens of Journal readers who responded to a question posed in this column two weeks ago. What can we do about the rising level of teen violence?

I heard from educators, academics, and police officers. All pretty much agreed that parents are the first line of defence, and should bear a greater responsibility to mould, mentor and monitor their children's behaviour.

Many Journal readers think the solution is simple. If possible, one parent should stay at home during their child's formative years, and employers and government should do more to support them.

A reader named Karen wrote, "Families would be healthier, and kids would feel like they belonged."

Other readers suggested today's parents are too quick to defend their children when they have problems with teachers, police or neighbours, and they want to see those parents held accountable for their children's actions — both financially and socially.

Maurice Brodeur is a constable with the Edmonton Police Service, and co-founder of a group called P.A.Y.V. — People Against Youth Violence.

"Schools don't have the ability to enforce accountability anymore because the parents back their kids to the nth degree, regardless of whether they are at fault or not. It's ridiculous."

Constable Brodeur likes a law in the U.S. dubbed the "Silverton Solution."

In 1995, the small town of Silverton, Oregon passed a bylaw that allows police to charge parents for the offence of "failing to supervise a minor." The courts can force parents to attend parenting training and/or pay restitution up to

4

$2,500 to people victimized by the child. The year before the bylaw was passed, there were 260 juvenile arrests. In 1995, that number dropped to 168, and 14 parents were cited for failing to supervise a minor.

Makes sense to me. But some Journal readers think we need to focus on the bigger picture. They argue that parents are no longer their children's primary role models.

Think about it. Teens today regularly see politicians get caught in lies on the six o'clock news. They watch corporate executives led away in handcuffs after bilking millions from their clients. What kind of message is that sending to today's youth?

"Media, parents, police, business leaders… everyone has a duty to live an honest life," says a Journal reader named Vickie. "Out of honesty will come decency, trust and respect."

University of Alberta criminologist Bill Pitt sees a distinct lack of respect and honour among some teens these days, and thinks there needs to be more of a deterrent factor.

"You should see what happens in juvenile court," Pitt explains.

"They're out in the hallways laughing at judges. There's no respect for the court system. They know they're not going to get anything. It's a real Wild West mentality."

More than a few Journal readers suggested a return to old-fashioned values. They want to see parents and schools teach a new millennium version of the Golden Rule — with a focus on respect, empathy, compassion, morals and ethics.

"We have deadened our moral intuition, and we are suffering from compassion fatigue," worries Sandra Woitas, a longtime Edmonton educator. So what do kids today need?

"One significant adult in their life… one friend. The ability to join a functional group… and each kid needs to find something they are good at. (Crime doesn't count.)"

Sandra feels the vast majority of teens today are good kids, and cautions the key to solving the problem of youth violence is not to lose hope.

"Hope is the oxygen of the human spirit."

Maybe we should all just take a few deep breaths. ■

The Quest For Instant Fame

So I'm riding out the great Edmonton blizzard of 2007 poolside in Palm Desert, California.

It's a glorious 73 degrees (23C), the palm fronds are fluttering in the breeze, and I'm thinking about the rich and famous.

The streets around here are named Frank Sinatra Drive, and Gene Autry Trail.

The cellphone cameras are flashing 20 minutes away in Palm Springs. Stars like Brad Pitt and Cate Blanchett are walking the red carpet at the International Film Festival.

We are fascinated with celebrities, so it's no surprise a new poll of 18- to 25-year-old Americans has discovered that their primary goal in life is to become rich and famous.

Pollsters from the Pew Research Center have dubbed them the "millennial generation" or Gen Y. A recent survey of 579 young people found that 81 per cent felt getting rich is their generation's "most important, or second most important" life goal. Fifty-one per cent said the same about being famous.

It's no wonder. The newsstands are filled with celebrity gossip magazines, breathlessly chronicling Britney Spears' every move. Who's she dating today — and more importantly — was she wearing underwear? Who cares? Millions of people, that's who.

Reality shows like Survivor, The Bachelor and American Idol turn ordinary people into overnight celebrities. One day you're working in a fast lube shop, the next you're getting VIP treatment at the best restaurants and bars in North America.

I think reality shows make today's teens pine for instant fame and notoriety. They're probably thinking, "Hey, all I have to do is be devious, or look really hot in a bathing suit and I can be a star too!" Work for a living? Why bother.

Problem is, even reality shows are not based on reality.

A couple of good friends produce reality TV for a living, and they admit to regularly manipulating the material to make the show more dramatic.

If a contestant is boring, the segment is cleverly edited to create tension that

---

didn't exist. Insert a shot of raised eyebrows here — take a better sound bite from earlier in the shoot and move it to another spot to make it "fit" better. I knew these shows were highly produced, but I naively thought they were for the most part "real."

So if we should be cynical about reality shows, we should also be cynical about the instant-fame they create, and the fallout. My advice to these spotlight-hungry wannabe stars is be careful what you wish for.

On the flight home from Palm Springs, the woman sitting next to me stared intently and finally asked, "Are you from St. Albert?" No, I smiled. She looked flummoxed.

"Are you famous?" she ventured.

No, I just work for Global News.

"Aha!" she said, "Well, you're famous to me!"

As a television news anchor, I always cringe when I'm asked to take part in a "celebrity" event. I'm no celebrity. I'm a journalist with 23 years experience. It just so happens that being on TV is a necessary part of the job.

The upside of having a higher profile is that people feel they know you. Total strangers are warm and friendly, often dispensing with the small talk, and blasting forward to deeply personal discussions in the lineup at Save-on-Foods. Within three minutes, they're telling you about a loved one who's dying of AIDS. It's pretty intense.

The downside is, people sometimes forget you're a real person with real feelings. They stand three feet away and talk about you like you're deaf. While the vast majority of people are kind and generous, a handful can be incredibly cruel, and it hurts.

I simply cannot imagine what it's like to be a "real" celebrity — your every move analyzed and criticized. You can't go outside in the morning to get the newspaper without the paparazzi trying to catch an unflattering photo. You gain 10 pounds and it's on the cover of US Weekly. Is being rich and famous really something to aspire to?

We all want to leave our mark on the world in some way... and fame's not necessarily a bad thing. But wouldn't it be better, and vastly more meaningful, to be famous for, say, finding a cure for cancer? Just wondering. ■

When Women Attack

What makes women want to tear apart other women? Are we so used to being held down that we can't resist sharpening our claws on the carpet — ready to pounce if another unfortunate female finds herself in a compromising situation?

Think about it. Millions of women around the world fawned over Martha's fruit flans, then chortled with delight to see Stewart headed to the hoosegow.

Hillary was pilloried during her tenure as first lady. Her female critics sniffed: "She's too pushy. Too involved. Secretly pines to be president."

Canada's first and only female prime minister Kim Campbell was vilified in the press. OK, she did pull that boneheaded move of posing nude behind legal robes — but still — she was making history, give her a break.

What about Deputy Prime Minister Anne McLellan, and Edmonton's only female mayor Jan Reimer? Critics snipe that their voices are "shrill and annoying."

This hyper-critical attitude extends to any woman in the public eye — no matter how "minor" their celebrity.

I just had lunch with a female co-worker, a talented young journalist. We compared notes about who had received the most outrageous hate mail from anonymous women. No kidding. Global News gets almost weekly phone calls, e-mails or snail mail from viewers immensely distraught about an on-air woman's hairstyle or wardrobe. We're talking seriously put out here — to the point of actually getting up, walking to the kitchen, finding the phone book, looking up the number, and asking to be put through directly to the offending female who dared get streaks in her hair, or voice an opinion that rankled.

Well here's a news flash folks: It hurts. Whether you're a newscaster, actress or politician — having a high profile doesn't mean you walk around with a cartoon force field that protects you from insults and attacks on your integrity. We're living, breathing people too and the anonymous criticisms can be deeply cutting. You try to rationalize them by telling yourself they're coming from strangers who don't know you and would never have the guts to say such hurtful things to your face.

Can you imagine being a "real" celebrity target like Britney Spears? Hoo doggie — get out the six-guns! That woman's breasts, wardrobe and romantic

4

exploits have been analyzed and criticized more than the Kyoto Accord. No wonder major celebrities often refer to themselves in the third person. I think it's a survival mechanism that allows them to protect their real psyche, while letting their "public" persona take the bullets.

So what drives women to be so nasty to each other? I will cop to having made some unflattering comments about other women on occasion. In my case, those comments were fueled by envy at times when my self-esteem tank was low. But I have never — not once — felt the need to actually reach out to a stranger and pass on a hurtful and hateful comment, because I know from first-hand experience what it feels like to receive one.

Case in point. I just received a typed letter at work marked "Personal and Confidential." No name, no return address. It began like this, and I quote: "We have read your column your (sic) staring (sic) in the Edmonton Journal & not too sure what your (sic) talking about most of the time. No one really gives a dam (sic) about you & your friends think. All you anchor people should really lighten up, your (sic) too serious & come across very snoody (sic). I think you better stick with your news job."

The author? An anonymous woman who says she's in her 50s.

Enter the "loonie jar." My female colleagues and I have come up with a creative way to deal with the anonymous criticism. Every time we get a nasty comment from a stranger we'll put a loonie in a jar until we have enough to go for pedicures.

Hmmm — turning poison into pampering. I like it. ■

Why Women Flash

Here's a question for all the women out there, no matter your age.

How much money would it take for you to lift your top and expose your breasts in public?

I'm not talking about parading around on a nude beach here. I'm talking about flashing thousands of people on a public street in broad daylight.

Would you do it for $1,000? $10,000? Would you do it for free?

Call me a prude, insecure, conservative, but I'm telling you right now, no amount of money would persuade me to go topless on a public street.

Throw in a half-dozen hurricane cocktails on Bourbon Street and I still wouldn't do it.

It's not that I'm morally opposed — I just don't see the point.

Is it the shock factor some women are after? A sense of power? Are they proud of their "assets" and want to show them off to the world?

"For some women it's fun to break the rules."

Mary Valentich is a certified sex therapist and professor in the faculty of social work at the University of Calgary.

She was intrigued last hockey season, when women started lifting their tops during the Stanley Cup playoffs in support of the home team Calgary Flames. Intrigued, because flashing is not common behaviour for most women.

Professor Valentich wanted to know why they did it, so she spent her own money on a study to find out.

After interviewing a handful of female flashers from the so-called Red Mile along 17th Avenue, the researcher was surprised by the wide range of motivations.

For some, it was simply about having a good time — a titillating way, if you will, to show support for the home team.

Others were intoxicated by the instant celebrity. They were dubbed the

"Flames Girls," their photos posted on Red Mile inspired websites for the entire cyber-world to see. It was their 15 minutes of fame.

The flashers were not all young either. Professor Valentich interviewed a 75-year-old woman who got caught up in the excitement.

"She came close to lifting her top. This woman felt a great comradeship with the others, and was quite ready to take it off. She simulated doing that with a scarf."

Some female flashers on the Red Mile felt powerful. They knew they had the crowd's attention and it made them feel good.

For others, it was a clear-cut political statement. If men can go shirtless, why can't they?

No matter the motivation, there's apparently no shortage of women looking for an opportunity to bare their boobs.

When a film crew for the Girls Gone Wild series came to Edmonton last year, about 1,000 people lined up outside a south-side nightclub, many of them women eager to lift their tops for the production crew. The American cameraman said it was the biggest lineup they'd ever seen for an episode of the X-rated series.

And therein lies the contradiction.

Many women argue for the right to be treated like men, saying breasts should not be sexualized by society. But their argument is watered down by the women who wield their sexuality like a weapon, using their bodies to gain power and prestige.

It's a complicated and confusing debate.

After wrapping up her research, Professor Valentich admits to having more questions than conclusions.

Like, what is healthy sexual expression? Valentich says young women these days are looking for wholesome ways to present their bodies without being judged, or taken advantage of. Good luck.

Part of me admires the Flames Girls' confidence and chutzpah, especially the 75-year-old would-be flasher.

But really... some things are better left to the imagination, don't you think? ■

Promiscuity

I feel sorry for little girls these days. They're being forced to grow up so quickly.

When I was eleven or twelve, I was riding horses in the bush, floating on inner tubes at the lake, or singing into a hairbrush as my favorite K-Tel record scratched away in the background.

Wide leg pants and plaid bush jackets were all the fashion rage. Most of my girlfriend's sported mousy brown mullets, and the occasional flash of blue eye shadow, secretly applied in the school bathroom.

It was an innocent time. Sure we pined over boys, but for the most part, it was all fantasy and no action. Only a handful of girls were even wearing training bras back then. We were kids on the cusp of becoming young ladies.

Today's little girls are maturing more quickly, getting their periods as young as age nine.

They're shopping for bras and even thong underwear at an earlier age, and dressing more provocatively to emulate their teenage idols on the red carpet.

Young girls are acting more like young women, giving a premature kick-start to their hormonal tanks. Maybe that's why young women are starting to behave more like young men these days.

I was shocked when a 20-something male colleague described the current bar scene. He lamented that women are becoming more predatory. Like men, they scope out the room, choose their target, and make a bold proposition.

"Let's go out to your car and get it on. You game?"

I couldn't believe it. He insisted it was true, and instead of being titillated by the offer, said the sexual boldness was actually a turnoff.

I thought his experience had to be an anomaly. But the more I asked, the more I heard about women increasingly becoming the sexual aggressor. Another male friend confessed to being approached in bars on several occasions by young women offering sexual favours. And here's the kicker. He's married - they knew it - and didn't care. Interesting.

Then there's the young businessman about town who claims to routinely receive naked photos on his cell phone from young women lobbying for a date. Honestly, get some self-respect ladies.

Melanie Beres is a PhD who studied gender psychology at the University of Alberta. She wrote her thesis on sexual consent, using seasonal workers in Jasper as her study group.

"There certainly does seem to be a trend where some women are actively seeking sex," agrees Beres.

The anti-rape activist and educator thinks the trend is linked to an increasing focus on women's sexual pleasure over the past decade or two. Hit shows like Sex in the City, and Girl's Gone Wild, portray young women taking control of their lives, deciding, when, where and who they want to be intimate with.

"It has become more acceptable for women to participate in previously taboo activities. On principle, I think this is good."

But while Beres thinks women should be free to explore their sexual desires, she says the reality is, they're still running into that age-old double standard. Young men who took part in her study said the best sex they ever had was with women who were assertive and up front about what they wanted. Yet those same men described that aggressive sexual behaviour as "slutty" and "unattractive". I guess it's one thing to do the dirty with an anonymous and willing partner, and quite another to bring her home to meet the parents.

And here's another interesting observation Beres made during her two-month study in Jasper. Despite some women's aggressive approach to casual sex, Beres says many admitted that, "sex seemed to be the 'cost' in order to get what they wanted – kissing, cuddling, companionship (even if just for one night)."

Ah, now it all makes sense.

I guess young women today aren't really all that different from women of my generation.

Despite their sometimes promiscuous behaviour, women are still really searching for the two "R's".

Romance and respect. ■

4

An Ethical Dilemma

So you're jogging down a back alley and you see something poking out of the quackgrass. You bend down to take a closer look, and discover it's a canvas bank bag with several bundles of 20-dollar bills inside. What do you do? Call the police? Or stuff the cash inside your track jacket and figure "finder's keepers" this is your lucky day?

I used to work as a teller in a small town Alberta bank. On the big mill and mine paydays we would literally empty the vault, as hundreds of young men lined up to cash their paycheques. On more than one occasion I was asked to get into my own vehicle and drive several miles to a competing financial institution to purchase 100 thousand dollars worth of twenties. I would stand at the counter, count the bundles, and then stuff them into my purse, occasionally stopping off for lunch at a restaurant before heading back to work.

Some people wondered why I didn't just hit the highway and keep going. But to me, they were just dirty stacks of paper, and besides, who wants to live life on the run?

Now you might think differently, but it's a fascinating point of discussion. If you'd like to get to know someone better, ask what they'd do with a big bag of cash that doesn't belong to them. I guarantee the answer will be revealing.

Or try this dilemma on for size… What would you do if someone bought you a lottery ticket and you won? Would you feel compelled to share the prize money?

My neighbour Glen was on the golf course one summer with his colleagues and some clients when they stopped for a beer. His business partner bought the round, and when the men cracked open their Coors Light cans, a funny sound caught everyone's attention. Turns out my neighbour had opened one of those talking beer cans. His prize? A brand new Oldsmobile. Glen was delighted and wrapped a red bow around the sports car for his wife's birthday. His business partner was not so thrilled, and sullenly listened to Glen's gleeful recounting of the big win to friends and neighbours.

What would you do? Offer to sell the car and split the money with your business partner – or keep the car for yourself? Many people I've asked said they would keep the prize, and buy the colleague a steak dinner to say thanks. There's no right or wrong answer here, but it makes for an interesting debate.

Finally, what if a friend bought you a 50/50 ticket at the football game and you won? It happened to my colleague Fraser Hiltz last year.

He arrived at the game late with friends, and the crowd was already roaring, so they were in a hurry to get to their seats. His friend's wife Sheila wanted to stop for 50/50 tickets, so while her husband headed for the stands, Fraser waited for her, and in return she shoved a "lucky" ticket in his pocket to say thanks. Fraser wasn't paying attention when the PA announcer read off the winning numbers, but Sheila was, and "her" ticket was just one number off.

She banged on Fraser's shoulder, "Check your ticket!"

He pulled the crumpled ticket out of his pocket, and sure enough, he had won. A 27-thousand dollar jackpot.

"I jumped up in disbelief," recalls Fraser, "and right away said that Sheila had to come down to the media centre with me because half of this was hers."

The next week Fraser wrote Sheila a personal cheque for $13,500.00. And he didn't stop there. Each of his daughters got one thousand dollars, his two sisters received 750 dollars each, and thirteen hundred went to a school breakfast program supported by his church.

"Just enjoying it all with them was fun."

What would you have done? Kept the cash for yourself – or shared your good fortune?

Again, there's no right or wrong answer here, but I think we could all learn something from Fraser's generosity.

If what goes around really does comes around, I think he may be in for some sweet karmic payback in the future. ■

Lynda's Life Lessons

I may be middle aged, but I still remember the excitement of my high school graduation.

The corsage — the group photos on my parents' front lawn — the sea of powder blue polyester and ruffles (and I'm talking about the guys here).

It's been nearly 30 years since I walked across the stage to get my high school diploma, and I've learned a thing or two since then that I'd like to share with the grads of 2007.

1. Find your passion in life.

   If you choose a job simply because it pays well, you'll end up bitter, bored and unfulfilled. If you do what you love for a living, you'll never "work" another day in your life.

2. Luck is "preparation meeting opportunity."

   Make your own luck. Don't sit back and resent others for getting ahead. Consider what they've done to make opportunities come their way, and realize that being "lucky" requires hard work and planning.

   If you lay the groundwork to achieve your goals, the "luck" that you envy in others will come your way eventually.

3. Life's no fun without taking calculated risks.

   I'm not talking about stunt driving or playing the stock market. I'm talking about taking on challenges that make you uncomfortable. Like standing up in front of hundreds of people to make a presentation, or maybe opening your own business someday.

   If you flatline your way through life, you may avoid some bumpy patches, but you'll also miss the big payoff - the thrill of taking a chance and succeeding beyond your own expectations.

4. There's no such thing as making a mistake, as long as you learn from it.

   We've all done dumb things in our lives. Instead of beating yourself up over it, figure out what you did wrong, and make sure it doesn't happen again in the future.

I've learned a lot more from my failures than my successes.

5. Spend less time worrying about what others think.

Be an original, walk on the wild side, be true to yourself and embrace your individuality.

Worry about real stuff, like am I a good person? Honest, fair, compassionate? How can I be a better son/daughter, friend, employee?

6. Think before you open your mouth.

If you force your opinion on others all the time, your words have less weight.

If you pick your battles carefully, people will be anxious to hear what you have to say when you do choose to speak.

7. Never stop learning.

Challenge yourself to learn something new every week.

Never pass up an opportunity to grow, whether it's taking on a special work project, or taking up a new hobby. Your efforts will be rewarded personally and professionally.

8. Your happiness is your responsibility.

If you're not happy in your personal relationships, then change them. Get rid of the toxic people in your life.

If you're not happy with the job you chose — then do something about it.

Analyze the situation, look for solutions and take action.

It's not up to your parents, your friends or your boss to make sure you're happy.

It's up to you.

9. Love your family and nurture your friendships.

If you're lucky, you'll still be in touch with maybe two friends from high school 25 years from now.

But your family will always be there for you and you will grow to appreciate their support even more, as life begins to throw you a few curve balls.

10. Respect your elders.

When I was 18 I thought I knew it all. When I was 30 I thought I mostly had it figured out. The older I get, the more I realize I've still got a lot to learn about life and relationships.

Learn from the people who have walked the path before you… respect them. Because someday — and sooner than you could ever imagine — you're going to be old too. ■

4

Photo illustration by Randall Scott, Global Edmonton Graphics Dept.

Finding Your Passion

If I could be anyone in the world for a fantasy 24 hours, I'd be a hockey player in the seventh game of the Stanley Cup playoffs.

Not just any player. I want to be the captain. I want to score the winning goal — feel the spray of champagne on my face in the dressing room, the ecstasy overriding exhaustion. I want to experience the joy, the pride, the brotherhood.

I want the fantasy to end the second the champagne hangover begins.

It's never going to happen, but that's OK, my real-life job is a bit of a fantasy too.

4

Twenty-three years ago I sat down in my first broadcast journalism class at college and had an epiphany. THIS is exactly what I was meant to do. I had found my passion. I still feel that way today, and it makes me sad to see how many people trudge through their days, eyeballing the clock desperate for their shift to end.

We need to work to pay the bills, but why settle for a job that bores you? Life is so much more interesting when you actually enjoy what you do for a living.

I've flown in the tail of the world's largest transport plane to Ukraine to produce a documentary for the CBC, gowned up to watch brain surgery on a young girl suffering from debilitating seizures, interviewed some of rock's bad boys of the 80s, Motley Crue and Ozzy Osbourne.

I've met premiers and prime ministers, reported live from the floor of the No campaign headquarters in Montreal during the 1995 referendum. I've ridden in the back seat of a police car during a high-speed call, watched paramedics literally pump the life back into a near-dead stabbing victim, sweated my way through choking forest fires and toured some of the toughest prisons in North America.

The best part? I got paid to have these amazing experiences.

The motivational speaker Dale Carnegie once said that in order to be truly successful in life, you have to find your passion. I think that's true. And it's never too late.

The key lies in identifying what really turns you on, then finding creative ways to make your passion literally pay off.

That might mean surviving a few crap jobs along the way to help you realize what you really don't like doing.

I partially financed my college education by working as a barmaid in the campus pub. At exactly 4 p.m. the cafeteria turned into a nightclub with 350 people demanding a drink RIGHT BLOODY NOW! I quickly discovered I don't like serving obnoxious people.

Speaking of bloody... my worst job was probably doing data entry at a Vancouver slaughterhouse. The ever-present stench of death was sickening. The monotony was broken occasionally by a sales guy coming into the steno pool to offer up a platter of the latest meat product skewered on toothpicks. Urp... no thanks.

I know what it's like to work only for the paycheque, and believe me, it's so much more rewarding to spend the day doing something that's challenging and interesting.

So if you're in high school and still not sure what to do for a living, spend some time seriously considering your fantasy job. Do you love music but know you'll never be a rock star? Consider taking courses that lead you to a career in the recording industry.

You're going to spend the better part of your adult life at work, so make your choices carefully.

Maybe you're retired and think the idea of passion in your life is irrelevant? Wrong.

Have you always wanted to take up a martial art? Become a gourmet cook? Learn how to play the drums? Do it now. You clearly have the time.

To all of you who are lucky enough to be living your passion right now, I salute you.

To those of you who haven't found your passion yet. Start looking. Today. ■

4

You Don't Look A Day Over...

5

Cougars

cougar / ˈkuːg3r / n. N. Amer. A large powerful tawny brown cat formerly widespread in the Americas but now reduced in number or extinct in many areas. (Courtesy: Mirriam-Webster's Collegiate Dictionary Tenth Edition).

cougar / ˈkuːg3r / n. A pathetic older woman prowling nightclubs and lounges looking for a relationship with a much younger man. (Courtesy: Global Television studio crew).

The word cougar fires up my eye twitch. I hate the word, and every female friend and colleague of mine over the age of 30 hates it, too.

Sorry boys, but when I go out for a drink with my 40-something girlfriends, I'm looking for a good glass of sauvignon blanc, not a vapid interaction with 20-somethings wearing low-rise baggy pants and high-top running shoes. I'm happily married to Kevin Bacon's doppelganger, a man with the physique of a 25-year-old and the mind of a mid-40s academic. So if I occasionally hit the hot spots without my husband, I'm relaxing, not prowling.

I not only hate the word cougar, I'm confused by it. Cougar can be the ultimate insult. "Hey, look at that cougar over there in the tight leather pants, lock up your boys tonight!" Or it can be a back-handed compliment. "Man that Heather Locklear is such a cougar, I'd trade places with Richie Sambora any day!"

There's even a book on the subject, called Cougar: A Guide for Older Women Dating Younger Men, written by Valerie Gibson. She describes herself as a "pioneer cougar" who knows her subject matter intimately, after running through no less than five husbands, one 14 years her junior. A quick scan reveals such illuminating chapter titles as "Landing Your Prey," and "Pouncing With Panache."

There's an internet dating website called "gocougar.com." A good friend of mine moved to a new city a few years ago. Lonely and yearning for some company of the male persuasion, she decided to give Internet dating a try. On her first "go cougar" blind date, she met the fellow outside a coffee shop on a busy downtown street. He looked fairly normal, but within the first five minutes announced he loved smoking pot. Smoked pot every day. Even his parents smoked pot… in fact he was stoned right now! My girlfriend excused herself to go to the washroom, then bolted out the front door.

Date number two looked more promising. A Nordic god. Blond, tall, athletic physique. They had a lovely dinner. My girlfriend was feeling rather optimistic until her date announced he was married. Good grief.

Date number three was a computer tech with an addiction to television. He was also broke, lethargic and slightly parasitic in his behaviour. This "cougar cub" had a habit of coming up behind my friend in the kitchen, draping his arms around her neck, and then literally hanging there while she tried to prepare dinner. The relationship finally ended in a public market, when my professional, zen-like girlfriend finally aimed a small squash-like vegetable at the parasite's head, bringing the short - but dull - Internet dating adventure to an end.

I'm sure Demi Moore had a very different experience when she first met her "boy toy" Ashton Kutcher. Or how about Madonna, and her "cub" husband Guy Ritchie, 10 years her junior. Do these women qualify as celebrity cougars?

Let's look at the other side of the equation. What about 60-year-old Michael Douglas marrying 35-year-old actor Catherine Zeta Jones? Is he a dirty old man? Simply lucky? Why is there no derogatory term to describe older men on the prowl for younger women? Personally, I like the word hyena.

Whoever came up with the word cougar anyway? I tried finding the answer on the internet. What I found instead was an interesting website called Quizilla. It invites you to fill out a questionnaire called "What Is Your Animal Personality?" After answering a handful of personal questions, the computer spit out my "true" animal destiny. Apparently I'm a badger. No explanation given.

Hmm, suddenly cougar doesn't sound so bad after all. ■

Embracing The Big 4-0

Oprah said something profound the other day that had me running for a pen and paper.

"When you're 32 you start to come into yourself. When you're 35, you're totally there."

Amen Oprah — and a pox on all you twenty something's who think that life ends at 30.

I once wasted an evening talking to a male colleague who was bemoaning the fact that at the age of 29, the "best years" of his life were over. That once he hit 30, he would "officially be old," his career would be on the "downslide".

I stared at him and thought two things.

1. You're an idiot.

2. Get over yourself, and get on with the business of living and learning.

I mean, get real.

When you're in your twenties you're just starting to figure out who you are and what you want out of life.

As a 22-year-old cub reporter, I had lots of chutzpah, energy and a good work ethic. That helped make up for the fact that I had absolutely no idea what I was doing.

The writing, interviewing, reporting and anchoring skills? Those came years later after slogging it out in the trenches.

At 30 you're still young, but old enough to be taken seriously. You're physically fit, wrinkle free, and financially independent. You have a pretty good idea of where you're going and how to get there. It's a time to begin building your legacy.

Consider:

Wayne Gretzky was mere months away from the big 3-0 when he broke Gordie

Howe's record for the most career points scored in the NHL.

At 43, rocker Jon Bon Jovi is still hot, happily married and stinking rich with another world tour rumoured to get underway this year.

Oprah Winfrey is 51 and looks better than she did at 40. She's thin, beautiful, peaceful and powerful. Forbes magazine estimates her net worth at $1.3 billion this year.

At 65, Canadian author Margaret Atwood has published 25 volumes of poetry, fiction and non-fiction. Her most recent novel, Oryx and Crake was shortlisted for the 2003 Booker Prize.

Clint Eastwood is celebrating his 75th birthday next month with a shiny new Oscar on his mantle for best director. I get the feeling he's not done yet.

Clearly 30 is not the end. It's just the beginning. Ask Lori-Ann Muenzer.

The Edmonton legal secretary was 38 when she exploded onto the cycling track at the Athens Olympics last summer, capturing Canada's first-ever gold medal in the sport.

Even Muenzer admits it was a stunning achievement for a female cyclist closing in on 40.

"I am a dinosaur… a stegosaurus in the world of sport."

A middle-aged marathoner at the top of the Olympic podium? Maybe. A sprint cyclist closing in on 40 blowing away competitors half her age? Improbable. But age is irrelevant to Lori-Ann Muenzer.

"I think it's just a number on your driver's licence. Age is what you believe it to be. I have to think about how old I am because I don't feel 38. Age has never been a factor."

Her motto? Plan it. See it. Believe it. Go out and achieve it.

That "never say die" mentality makes Muenzer a brilliant choice as ambassador of the upcoming World Master's Games in Edmonton.

Over 16,000 athletes from 100 countries will compete here in July. The minimum age to register for most Master's sports? 30.

If you're tempted to sign up, but think you're too old to go for the gold... Lori-Ann has a message:

"If you've got a dream, go out and go for it. You've got nothing to lose, and don't let anyone tell you it's stupid, because if everyone had said to me don't start (cycling) when I was 28 — nobody would know my story, and I would have given up."

And if you think an Olympic gold medal at 38 is impressive — Lori-Ann's not done yet.

She's hoping for a gold medal repeat at the China summer Olympics in 2008. She'll be 43 by then. No one has ever won an Olympic gold medal in cycle sprints at the age of 43. But Muenzer's not daunted.

"Never say never, and don't say 'I can't'. Those are just a couple of words that should be taken out of the dictionary."

OK. 43 is one thing — but first things first. How does she feel about hitting the big 4-0?

"I love it. I'll be 39 in May. It's just another number. Maybe it means I'll have a bigger party."

That's one party I'd love an invite to. ▪

5

Laptop Diaries - You Don't Look A Day Over...

The GNO celebrates a decade = left to right KT, Lynda, KD, Mo & Sue)

Menopausal Lament

A sunset kayak to Chocolate Beach on Salt Spring Island, followed by a champagne toast under the stars to four of my favourite women on this earth.

My 10th annual girl's cabin weekend is in the history books. And for the first time in a decade, no one had to wear the infamous "crown of confusion" — the makeshift hat reserved for the person having the biggest personal or professional meltdown of the year.

No, 2005 has been a very good year for my girlfriends and I.

With no relationship crises, or work woes to talk about, we ventured into new conversational ground this summer… a subject all five of us are intimately familiar with. Perimenopause.

"Your PMS days are 10 times worse," my good friend Mo lamented. "The abdominal bloat comes around the corner before I do."

Perimenopause is a classic time of transition in a woman's life that usually manifests itself in the early to mid 40s, and can last up to a decade. Your ovaries decrease the amount of hormones they produce, wreaking all kinds of havoc.

5

"Have you ever woken up really hot and sweaty and drenched, your hair really matted?" Mo says... "Like I've had that for ten years."

Then there's the weight gain, headaches, sleep disruptions, skin changes, flagging libido, memory loss, fatigue, menstrual irregularities, bone loss. Add to that the emotional distress, crying jags, and flashes of white rage.

"There were times I wanted to rip somebody's head off and spit down the hole."

At the age of 44, my friend Kathy has been dealing with hormonal mood swings for a couple of years now.

"These frightful moments that just weren't me. I was so afraid of losing my sanity — hurting other people emotionally."

Then there's the whole sociological aspect of going through the change — "like going from a fertile, sexy female... to barren, brittle and invisible."

My friend KT says it's not the aging that bothers her... it's the loss of her sexuality.

"I don't want to feel shrivelled up. I don't want to have any more babies, but I want to be able to."

That mindset was captured on the cover of Time magazine a couple of years ago. The subject of menopause was illustrated by a photo of a wizened old tree.

Is that really the way society views women going through menopause?

My friend Mo shared this disheartening little anecdote... "A friend told me the day she turned 49 and she actually started going through menopause — like hot flashes — was the day she realized men were not looking at her anymore."

Too bad we don't live in Japan.

Women there don't experience menopause the way we do in North America. Many Japanese women have absolutely no symptoms. Researchers say it could be their soy-based diet. Or it could be that Japan's respect for older people makes the menopausal transition more comfortable. Instead of being seen as invisible, older women move into a place of great honour. Wouldn't that be nice?

Just as I was feeling rather hopeless about my looming lot in life, my friend Sue offered up this nugget of sunshine:

"My friends who've been through it are thrilled out of their minds. They said it's so fantastic… they feel lighter, sexually their lives are great because they never have to worry about getting pregnant again. They don't have symptoms anymore. They feel free."

So there may be a light at the end of the tunnel. Too bad we couldn't stop that particular train from arriving in the first place.

At least we're talking about it. But are we obsessing about it?

My friend Mo thinks we're a self-indulgent, whiney generation that eats up headlines like COPING WITH AGING. OUR FIRST HEART ATTACK. OUR MENOPAUSE.

"Why does it have to be a big deal at all?" Mo asks. "I think we should just shut up about it, and get over ourselves."

Ah, but that would be like our mother's generation. Millions of women forced to suffer in silence, with limited information about treatment options, and no understanding and compassion from family and husbands in particular.

I say we've come a long way, baby.

When they find a way to control the symptoms that won't kill us, THEN I'll shut up about it. ■

Facelifts And Fantasy

"Why is it that beautiful women never seem to have any curiosity?" Author Penelope Gilliatt first posed that question in 1967.

She said: "Ordinary, ugly people know they're deficient and they go looking for the pieces."

Well, nearly 40 years later, it seems even the most genetically gifted among us are on a surgical scavenger hunt for the key to everlasting beauty.

Take the hit show Desperate Housewives. Name aside, I was rather delighted to learn that three of the four lead actresses are in their 40s.

But instead of revelling in their success, these mid-life sexpots are being forced to bat away persistent rumours that they tweaked and tucked their way back into the prime-time spotlight.

Forty-one-year-old Nicollette Sheridan who plays the vampy Edie on Desperate Housewives was so incensed by the "malicious" gossip, that she hired a Beverly Hills plastic surgeon to examine her face and "prove" she was aging naturally.

In this looks-obsessed era of Extreme Makeover and The Swan I guess it's hard to believe that anyone over the age of 40 is a natural beauty who works out five days a week. Surely they had some high-tech help? A magic weight loss pill?

Maybe we've seen too much of Michael Jackson's nose. Maybe we've been numbed and stunned by the sight of all those lovely actresses who get their lips injected full of bum fat and all manner of chemical substances. In Hollywood it's called a "trout pout".

Men are not immune to the allure of plastic surgery either.

There's a guy in the States who's spent tens of thousands of dollars trying to look like Roseanne's ex, Tom Arnold. (OK, Jude Law maybe...)

An Edmonton plastic surgeon once told me about a male patient who came to his office pleading to be surgically transformed into the martial arts expert Bruce Lee. This guy wasn't even Asian. I think he needed a psychiatrist, not a surgeon.

5

Then there's the insane story of Manhattan socialite Jocelyne Wildenstein. She's spent more than my entire life's RRSP contributions on plastic surgery to make herself look like a cat. No kidding, slanted feline shaped eyes and the works. Whatever happened to the Hippocratic oath? Her doctor should be ashamed.

Having said that, there is some good news on the beauty battlefront to report.

A new survey by the magazine More discovered that women between the ages of 40 and 44 are more likely to feel better about their looks now than they did five years ago.

Once they hit 40, 64 per cent of women are pleased by what they see in the mirror. Of women under 40, only 42 per cent are pleased by their reflection.

Here's the bad news. That same survey found that "After the big Five-O, women feel less secure about their looks. At age 55, 45 per cent of women like what they see in the mirror; at 60, just 35 per cent."

I guess I'm right on the cusp. At 44, I'm fit, happy and healthy. I love my job and I've got the best husband in the world.

Yes, it's true I'm noticing a few more lines around the eyes, and no matter what I do, I've got an annoying little pooch of belly fat.

So truth be told, if a safe, fast, cheap, and painless way to shave five years off my appearance was developed I'd probably go for it.

Alright, I'd push you out of line to get it done first.

Until then — when it comes to aging gracefully, I'm going to give the last word to the always stunning actress Susan Sarandon.

She was recently quoted in More as saying "Do I rule out cosmetic surgery? I'm not going to say never. Usually the people who say they'll never do anything are 35 — so what do they know? The thing that stops me is that I just don't want to look like a burn victim. I'm almost 60, and I don't want to be 60 years old and look 20. There's something to be said for looking good but looking your age."

Amen. ■

Two Thumbs Up For Dove

Her nose is too thick – her lips a little too thin. She has sallow skin, acne, lank mousy brown hair, and slightly hooded eyes… not exactly the makings of a supermodel.

Yet thanks to a team of beauty experts, a blur of makeup brushes, curling irons, good lighting and some high tech wizardry, this extremely average young woman is transformed into a stunning cover girl before your very eyes.

Mind you, the metamorphosis includes some disturbing computer trickery. The model's neck is elongated, her brown hair turned blonde, eyebrows digitally lifted, eyes enlarged, and lips plumped to twice their original size. Presto! Billboard ready bombshell in under sixty seconds. Even her own mother wouldn't recognize her.

The video is called "Evolution". Over eight million people around the world have already checked it out on the web site Youtube.

The ad was created by the Dove skin care company in response to a survey in 2004 that found only 2 per cent of women around the world consider themselves to be beautiful. I find that very sad.

We're insecure and obsessed with perfection.

Dove researchers found that 92 per cent of girls aged 15 to 17 would like to change something about their appearance. They wish their hips were smaller, breasts bigger, noses more streamlined. They want to look like Lindsay Lohan, or whichever starlet the media deems hot at the moment.

I've been watching the Dove "real beauty" campaign evolve over the past couple of years. At first I was a bit cynical, thinking the focus on "real" women was a bit of a self-serving gimmick. Obviously it's cheaper to hire someone off the street, instead of a 10 thousand-dollar a day model. But Dove seems to be walking the walk.

"We're trying to reach women of all ages," says Alison Leung, Dove's Canadian marketing manager.

"We want older women to say it's ok to look your age, and that's beautiful… and we're trying to help young girls develop healthier, more realistic attitudes about appearance, weight and age."

Dove has developed several educational programs for girls to get them talking with Moms and other mentors about self-esteem. Educators can download free teaching resources from the company's web site, and a special fund provides support to organizations that treat eating disorders.

And as for those unrealistic media images that are impossible for the average woman to live up to? When it comes to casting calls for upcoming ad campaigns, Dove has a strict policy - no professional models.

Eileen Chan is a 28 year-old flight attendant from Edmonton. She went to a Dove casting call on a whim in 2005 and was chosen from among thousands to pose in her skivvies for a national ad campaign.

"It was a shock at first." Eileen laughs. "Wow that's a really big billboard and I'm in my underwear!"

Eileen was picked because she's a fun young Asian woman who's comfortable with her curves, and not afraid to show them off. She's proud of the message she helped convey.

"Love yourself no matter how you look. No matter how old, or whatever race you are... let that shine."

It's cool to see average people redefining beauty and fighting back against the ageist mentality that's held women back for so many years.

I'm tired of the media messages that insinuate women over 50 are worthless, washed up and unattractive. So I'm particularly interested in Dove's latest campaign. Instead of an anti-aging focus, it's putting a positive spin on getting older. The new "pro-age" campaign focuses on women over the age of 50.

I will sheepishly admit to feeling a slight twinge of discomfort the first time I saw the TV commercials. Grey haired women proudly posing in the nude. No special lighting - no makeup sleight of hand.

"Our goal is to portray a more realistic picture of aging," Alison Leung explains, "So people aren't shocked when they see what a real woman looks like."

Sadly, we've grown accustomed to seeing 18 year-old models pitching wrinkle creams.

We need to get real, and there's no better time like the present. More Canadian women will turn 50 this year than at any other time in history. ■

Lisa & Lynda celebrate a milestone

The 25 Year Class Reunion

One glance at my inbox and the synapses started firing. Subject line: 20 year College Reunion.

Intrigued and slightly horrified, I double clicked to find a group email addressed to the Class of '84 Broadcast Journalism students — were we interested in getting together in Vancouver to celebrate 20 years out of BCIT?

My mental Rolodex started twirling through blurry snapshots of another era.

I was 20 years old and 20 pounds overweight, sporting a Ms. Clairol blond mullet teased nice and high on top. A small town girl from Hinton, Alberta in a big city journalism program with 45 other broadcast wannabes.

Did I really want to relive this inauspicious era?

Class reunions play on your worst insecurities — fears about fat, wrinkles, baldness; the probing questions about who's now divorced, unemployed or maybe even gay.

There's the inevitable, if unspoken, competition. Who's the most successful? Who's the biggest failure? Who still looks good in their 40s? You can't help but compare yourself to your fellow classmates.

Then there's the fear factor involved in remembering who's who.

These days I walk into a room and can't remember why I'm standing there. How will I recognize people I haven't seen in two decades?

I keep in regular contact with exactly one former college classmate named Lisa. Our lives have taken us in different directions, both professionally and geographically, but we still rendezvous once a year for a girls' getaway weekend.

So we RSVP'd for the BCIT reunion, figuring if it was a bust we'd bail and still have the weekend together in Vancouver.

My heart was pounding when the cab dropped us off at the party. The face recollection was a bit fuzzy at first, but the room had a warm and welcoming vibe. We had history. We had all made an effort to be there, and we were genuinely interested in each other's lives. Within 15 minutes, I realized I was actually… having fun!

Not everyone made the reunion. My old roommate Corinne wasn't there. She was a petite and pretty woman with a ribald sense of humour. One year in college, she surprised us all by winning a yodelling contest in front of thousands of drunken Okoberfest revellers. Corinne took on cancer in her late 20s and lost her hair, but won the battle. Now she's raising a young family and couldn't make the trip.

The class clown wasn't there either, and we missed his dry wit. Turns out Brian had finally surrendered bachelorhood to become a family man. His wife was in hospital one night preparing to undergo a C-section, when Brian was found dead in his own bed, the silent victim of an undiagnosed heart condition. At the age of 45, my former classmate left behind a two-year-old son, and a newborn daughter he would never see. We had a teary toast in his honour.

When the party petered out, a small group of us ducked into an old Greek restaurant on Granville Street for a nightcap round of spicy Caesars and sausage pizza. It was close to 3 a.m. when we finally paid the bill and called it a night.

Bleary-eyed but still feeling giddy, Lisa and I walked back to our hotel, wiped off our makeup and crawled into bed, giggling and gossiping like school girls until sunlight started leaking through the hotel curtains.

It's been a long time since I pulled an all-nighter. Made me feel like I was 20 again. I highly recommend it. ■

Have You Seen My Reading Glasses?

When I was eight, I thought I'd test out this God thing. The school nurse had suggested I might have a vision problem, and wearing glasses seemed like a fate worse than death.

So that night in bed I gave it a whirl. "Dear God, if anyone's up there, please don't make me wear glasses!" Apparently he didn't hear me.

The next day the optometrist confirmed it. The diagnosis? Nearsighted. The remedy? Glasses. My first pair were small, gold rimmed ovals. I hated them passionately.

It took a while, but my little girl prayers were finally answered 30 years later. My visual salvation came in the form of three words — laser eye surgery.

It may seem somewhat irresponsible to slide your perfectly healthy eyeballs under a high-powered laser beam — but you have to understand — my window of opportunity was quickly closing. I was 38, just a few short years away from the hell that would be bifocals.

Optometrists say most of us will need reading glasses by the time we hit our mid-forties. It's a condition called presbyopia. The muscle fibres in the eye get progressively stiffer making it difficult to focus on close work like sewing, reading or using the computer.

The older you get, the longer you wish your arms were. It was clear if I wanted to experience the thrill of unfettered 20/20 vision — I had to take the plunge now.

So with some trepidation, and half a Valium at the Gimbel Eye Centre, I put my corneas in the hands of a young surgeon. It was the next best thing to a religious experience.

Imagine the joy of running outside in the river valley without your glasses fogging up in the winter; downhill skiing in Banff without the burn of mountain air drying out your contact lenses. It was frankly exciting just to wake up in the morning and be able to see the alarm clock.

20/20 vision was a heady experience. I played games with my TV co-anchor Gord during the commercial breaks. We'd get the studio cameramen to roll backwards farther and farther, as we competed to see who could still read the teleprompter. I always won.

My smugness evaporated three months ago, when I realized that five short years after laser eye surgery, my vision was becoming less eagle-eyed, and more Mr. Magoo-like. Turns out both eyes had degenerated, one slightly, one severely, giving me a condition called monovision. One eye sees distance, one sees close up. Some patients actually request this visual anomaly, because if you can get used to it, you'll never have to wear reading glasses.

But for me, monovision is like viewing life through a funhouse mirror — kind of sharp — but bizarrely distorted at the same time. I cannot live life like that. I want my clear vision back again.

Here's the problem. If I go under the laser again, I'll be able to read road signs — but I won't be able to read a book. The surgeon says based on my current age, I'll probably vault myself into the aggravating world of reading glasses.

I was introduced to this world recently at a restaurant with my sixtysomething parents. Both had forgotten their reading glasses, so I was forced to recite fifty odd menu items as they gently bickered about what to order and share.

"What was the house special again?"

"Does that come with fries?"

It was a weird role reversal, the child becoming parent.

Based on that little scene, reading glasses seemed like a very bad idea, but so did the concept of going back to contact lenses. They're uncomfortable and annoying. The other day I was in such a hurry at work, I actually popped both lenses into the same eye, then ran around like a nut thinking I'd dropped the "missing" lens on the office carpet somewhere.

That was it. I've booked the laser enhancement surgery for next Thursday. I'm nervous about it, but they make funky reading glasses these days don't they? ∎

What Was Your Name Again?

When you work in the media, you meet a lot of people. It's both a blessing and a curse.

I've interviewed literally thousands of people in the past 20 years — farmers, politicans, police officers, authors, athletes, and the list goes on.

It's fun to be exposed to so many new people all the time. The trouble is, I can't remember their names, and the older I get, the more my memory banks fail me.

My husband and I were out for dinner with another couple recently, when some friends unexpectedly dropped by the table to say hi. I was alternately delighted to see them, then mortified to realize I could not recall one of their names. The couple we were sitting with waited expectantly for an introduction, while I secretly prayed my surprise table guests would say a quick hello and then move along swiftly enough that my rudeness would be overlooked. No. The two couples quickly discovered common ground about a recent vacation destination, and chatted animatedly for several minutes as I died a slow death of embarrassment.

It's not just a recall problem. Successfully remembering names means you have to actually "hear" them in the first place.

I don't know about you, but I'm a visual person. I look first — listen later.

When I'm first introduced to someone new, I'm absorbed with taking in their whole being, looking at their face, their clothing, noting their height, body language, smile, everything really… except their name.

Self-improvement guru Dale Carnegie once said, "A person's name is to that person, the sweetest most important sound in any language."

I believe it. That's why I'm determined to do something about my name retention problem. So I've been doing a little research.

Franklin D. Roosevelt was renowned for his ability to remember the name of just about every person he met. His secret? The late U.S. President would look at the person he was being introduced to, and imagine their name written across their forehead. Then when he later recalled their face — lo and behold! There was the person's name as well. This technique apparently works even better if you imagine the name written with a coloured felt pen.

I tried it the other day at a company sales event. After being introduced to a colleague from Toronto, I stared intently at his forehead and mentally scrawled A-D-A-M with a bright red Jiffy Marker. For the rest of the afternoon, every time he walked past me I had to smile, envisioning this top-level executive with his name displayed on his forehead. OK, that seems to work. Now what about the hundreds of people I've already met but didn't employ the felt pen technique at the get go? Worse yet, what about those people I've met so many times I bloody well should know their names, but now am too embarrassed to ask?

Let's face it, people are insulted if you forget their name, so how do you gracefully recover? Some people opt for good old honesty.

"I must be losing it, but for the life of me, I can't remember your name right now."

Others try a clever deception.

"I'm so sorry, I've forgotten your name." 'It's Diane.' "Oh, I know your first name is Diane, I meant I couldn't remember your "last" name." Good one.

There's the fishing expedition method.

"Wow, it's been a long time… where did we run into each other last?"

Hopefully you'll dig up a clue that leads to the forgotten name.

You can always employ the old spouse "switch and bait" tactic. If you don't introduce your partner in the first 10 seconds, it means they're supposed to thrust out their hand and introduce themselves.

"Hi, I'm Lynda's husband Norm. What was your name again?"

(Note: this only works if your significant other remembers they have a role to play in the name retrieval gambit.)

If you have a surefire method of remembering and recalling names, I'd love to hear it.

In the meantime, I'll be giving my mental Jiffy Marker a serious workout. ∎

Help... I'm Losing My Mind

I am slowly but surely losing my mind, and I'm more than a little peeved.

I used to fancy myself a quick-witted conversationalist, capable of holding a cocktail crowd rapt with a witty story or two. But these days I've been known to stop mid-gesticulation and splutter, "What the @%!!&*# am I talking about?" A few helpful word prompts later, and I'm back on my storytelling way. It's embarrassing, and more than a little aggravating.

It seems my brain cells are gradually winking out one by one, the residual puff of smoke clouding my once-trusty memory banks. I'm often left searching for, the ah, um... appropriate word... and marching purposefully down the hallway to... well... hmm... what the heck am I doing here again? Arggh — I'll remember by the time I get back to my desk.

My only solace is in knowing I'm not alone. A quick survey of friends and relatives unearthed several mortifying — yet amusing — memory-loss moments. Like the time my parents attended a banquet in Hinton. My dad was president of the local chamber of commerce. He gave a lovely welcoming speech to the crowd, then proceeded to introduce the head table. My mom says, "He was doing a wonderful job until he came to me. HE COULD NOT REMEMBER MY NAME. I had to help him out amid an explosion of laughter."

Ah Dad, sadly, I can relate.

My friend was at a party recently when he launched into a complicated joke that petered out when he forgot the punchline. Humiliated, he said "I spent the next 45 minutes of the party smiling and nodding like I was engaged in the conversation, but all the while I was actually doing mental gymnastics trying to jog my memory on the joke that had fallen flat." Been there.

The older you get the more brain cells you lose, and your body produces less of the chemical needed to boost the brain cells you have left. It's a universal condition. Aging changes the way the brain stores memory, making it harder to recall information and the ability to remember gets worse with each passing year.

I've tried memory tricks, like turning my ring around to remind myself of an important appointment or task. That worked for years, until I couldn't remember why I turned the ring around in the first place.

My girlfriend juggles three young children, a husband, volunteer work and a part-time career. She used a colour-coded dot system on a refrigerator calendar to keep track of everyone's appointments. That ended one day when she said, "I noticed a couple of these dots on the back of my daughter's shirt and freaked out. Where are these from? What if I miss something? Why do you have to walk so close to the damn fridge?"

Now she uses coloured highlighter pens.

I myself am the Queen of Post-It notes. My kingdom is filled with yellow sticky reminders on my computer (live newsbreak times), my desk blotter (meeting Tuesday), my bathroom mirror (hair appt. tonight), my door (bring lunch), my counter (Hi Dear - dinner tonight at 8?).

If Post-It notes aren't your thing, geriatric experts suggest:

- Make lists of things you need to remember.

- Get enough sleep — the brain needs a good eight hours to function properly.

- Butt out — smokers forget people's names more than non-smokers.

- Keep learning — a daily mental workout helps keep the brain strong.

- If you have to remember a phone number, say it out loud. The more you say it, the greater your chances of remembering it.

- Use mental associations. If you meet someone new named Ralph, try picturing him as the premier. It'll help you recall his name in the future.

Finally — take heart. The Alliance for Aging Research predicts that in less than 10 years a magic memory pill will be discovered that will be "one of the great joys of the baby boomers."

Great. Then we'll just have to remember to take it. ■

Musical Memories

Play a tune by the 80's pop group Little River Band, and I'm immediately transported back in time to a hormone-fueled romp across B.C.

I'm a 19-year-old bank teller. He's a handsome oil rigger named Chip with a shiny new maroon coloured Trans Am.

We're on a weeklong road trip to Vancouver, and Little River Band is the soundtrack to our fast-forward, titillating teenage romance.

Noel Coward was right when he said: "Extraordinary how potent cheap music is."

Motown is the magic elixir for Edmonton Mayor Stephen Mandel. Bands like The Temptations and the Four Tops.

A few bars of My Girl will send Mandel on a stroll down memory lane in Windsor, Ontario.

Mandel and his teenage friends would drive across the Ambassador bridge into Detroit to hear the great Motown bands of the era play live.

"It reminds me of my youth… the spirit of it. It was a simpler time, a youthful time… and it still moves me today."

Music evokes powerful memories, both good and bad.

My co-anchor Gord Steinke used to make his living as lead singer and bass player in a rock band.

He remembers playing a nightclub in Hamilton, Ontario when, "Two midgets got into a fight on the dance floor in front of me. They were arguing over a tall, pretty blond who was dancing with both of them. I was singing Brown Sugar by the Rolling Stones, when to our horror one of the midgets pulled out a knife and stabbed the other one. To this day every time I play Brown Sugar those terrifying images come flooding back."

Most of our strongest musical memories are formed in our youth, according to the director of Harvard University's Institute for Music and Brain Science, Dr. Mark Jude Tramo.

"There's a time in your life when you're more vulnerable to having imprints made emotionally. It's when you're not settled down — haven't developed a career or monogamous relationship. It's a special time in life."

Dr. Tramo says the music video is changing the way young people store and process musical memories.

If you're over 40, you grew up listening to your favourite bands on the radio. It's a different story for kids today.

"Now young people are reared on MTV or VH1 as opposed to records," Dr. Tramo says, "Where the song… you can't release it without the video. So there's a whole new generation of people who will typically have a memory for a song that has the visuals to go along with it."

I don't know about you, but I'd rather listen to a tune and dream up my own mental images, than be force-fed visuals of Shania Twain as a sci-fi temptress on a space-age hog — or Robert Palmer's back-up band of red lipped zombie models. Regardless of your generation, the musical memories stored in your youth will stay with you until the day you die.

Alzheimer's may rob you of the ability to remember your own children's names — but your decades-old musical memories will still be fresh.

"Some memories are very stable." Dr. Tramo says, "You may not be able to learn new songs, but the memories you have already laid down are strong. With Alzheimer's patients, you can play them old songs, and it will make them happy instead of depressed. Memories are stable even in the face of disease."

Some day when I'm old and confused, I hope they wrap me up in a crocheted blanket and play a few tunes from Little River Band. That's guaranteed to put a smile back on my face. ■

Time Is Flying By

Ever feel like your life is racing away?

The older I get, the faster the days fly by. Here it is Friday… again.

Christmas is only 23 days away. I'm scrambling to shop, put up the tree, send cards, string the lights… again.

Didn't I just do this? What happened to fall? Did we actually have a summer this year? Why is time going so bloody fast?

When I was a kid growing up in the foothills of Hinton, each day stretched into a delicious eternity.

We'd pretend we were on horseback, galloping through the bush for hours on some fantasy adventure. A can of creamed corn was cooked up for lunch on a rusted-out camp stove in the local park.

At nighttime, the neighbourhood kids played hide-and-seek until it was so dark you couldn't make out the faces anymore. Even then we were reluctant to come inside.

The weekend seemed to last forever. The Disney theme music on Sunday night was the only thing that pulled you back to reality, with the sinking feeling in your gut that you actually had to go to school the next morning.

"Kids and adults do time estimation differently."

Dr. Anthony Chaston is a former psychology professor from the University of Alberta, who now teaches at Keyano College in the heart of oil country, Fort McMurray.

His PhD research explores the mysterious field of time perception. Why do children and adults experience time in such vastly different ways?

"The little kid isn't worried about the global world, like time management. He's a little kid. He lives in the moment. He's just going about doing his thing. So retrospectively, time must pass slowly for them."

Children also store rich memories of their daily escapades, and those memories trick the child's brain into thinking they spent a lot of time on the task at hand. Ergo — the endless day.

"Whereas as adults, we live in this world of clocks, and we have to be aware of time all the time." Dr. Chaston explains.

"So as adults, our time estimates, and our perception of the passage of time are probably more centred around the idea that we're monitoring it all the time."

The theory? Focus on the clock and time goes by more quickly.

This is not encouraging news. I work in a profession that lives and dies by the clock.

Deadlines every half-hour. Script assistants who count literally every second that goes into the 6 o'clock news. I have a wristwatch — a desk clock — a timer on my computer.

I am OBSESSED with time. No wonder my life is racing away like cartoon calendar pages in a windstorm.

But there is hope, even for me.

Dr. Chaston says a lot of human time estimation is based on what you "remember" doing. So the key is — if you "remember" more, you "feel" like you've had a more rich experience, which makes you feel like you're really living your life, not just watching it whiz by.

"It's the old cliche… if we stop and smell the flowers, and we reflect upon what we're doing, research shows you get a much more rich memory representation of what you did."

Is it really that simple?

Psychologists admit they don't have all the answers when it comes to time perception.

The brain is still largely a mystery to the medical community, so there's some guesswork involved in understanding why life seems to speed up as we get older. But Dr. Chaston says we should take comfort in knowing we're not alone, and he offers up this last bit of advice on slowing your life down this Christmas season.

"If you have too many things going on, then everything is rushed, and you don't really reflect upon your experiences. Just engaging in your life is really the most simple thing that might work."

Hmmm. I smell a new year's resolution coming on... ■

5

Santa's On The Way

6

New Year's Resolutions

The worst New Year's resolution I ever made was to quit smoking. Good idea, bad execution. It was exactly five minutes after midnight when I lit up again, losing a $50 bet to my teenage boyfriend. Fifty dollars was a lot of money in those days — still is actually.

Losing the cash was bad enough. You should have seen what he spent it on. A tattoo the size of a cigarette package. My 17-year-old coal miner suitor peeled back a bloody bandage on his left bicep to reveal an eagle holding a scroll in its claws. A scroll with my name inside, printed in bold black letters. Yeah, no pressure there. Years after our teenage romance fizzled, my former boyfriend added injury to insult by having my name squiggled out in black tattoo ink.

It wasn't the only well-intentioned resolution that was made in earnest and not quite achieved. Like many people, I've vowed not to sweat the small stuff, to stop being frustrated by things I have no control over. I've resolved to apologize when I've done someone wrong, and forgive others instead of holding a grudge.

New Year's resolutions are really about recognizing your flaws, and making a commitment to do something about them. I guess I'm a constant work in progress.

Apparently I've got a lot of company in the failed resolutions department — a lot of "female" company it seems. Most women I know have made at least a few hopeful and healthy resolutions in their lifetime. Eat more apples and fewer french fries. Log more miles on the treadmill. Stop buying clothes you don't need and can't afford. Dump the energy sucking boyfriend. Learn how to deal with stress before the meltdown. Volunteer more often. Noble and altruistic goals. So why do we fail so often?

It could be that resolutions are a bit like asking the plastic eight ball oracle for the answers to life's big questions. We get a kick out of the process — but do we really believe in the answer? More importantly, are we willing to put in the hard work that's necessary to make those December 31st wishes come true?

Some experts in the field of human behaviour insist New Year's resolutions are a waste of time. John Assaraf calls himself one of the leading optimum performance experts in the world. He claims resolutions are based on willpower. Problem is, he says willpower is controlled by your conscious mind, and 90 per cent of your behaviour and perception is controlled by your unconscious mind. Assaraf says people don't understand how their brains work, so they renege on their resolutions 99 per cent of the time — a depressing statistic.

I'm no expert on human behaviour, but I recently did a straw poll at work. Of the 10 women asked, all had made at least one New Year's resolution in their lifetimes. Of the 10 male colleagues surveyed… one had vowed to quit smoking, and failed. The other nine had never bothered to make a resolution in the first place.

Why not? The answers ranged from the simple "What for?" to the practical "I know my limitations. My willpower is weak." But others had a very interesting, and very male take on the yearly custom. Why set a specific day to begin making your life better? Why not resolve to change things starting right now? One male colleague summed it up this way. He said "today is the first day of the next year of my life. If I need to clean up my act, I resolve to do it right now — why wait until December 31st"?

You know, I think he may be on to something there.

By the way, you may be interested to know I've finally managed to quit smoking after my failed resolution 25 years ago. I quit about 10 times actually before beating the seductive cancerous demon into submission. But truth be told, if you offered me an aromatic cigarillo on New Year's Eve around midnight, I might still be tempted to light up. 2004 New Year's resolution? Quit smoking for good, no cheating, no excuses. ▪

Christmas Is Relaxing...
(If You're A Guy)

Men are either extremely lazy or extremely clever when it comes to Christmas shopping. Every year at this time, women are on the verge of mall rage, while their husbands and boyfriends find other more relaxing things to do with their time.

Why is it "women's work" to battle the frenzied holiday crowds? It's a finely aged yuletide whine. Men dodge responsibility by wheedling "you're better at it than I am." Or "I don't know what to get my mother."

Well neither do we, but women buy these lame excuses year after year, knowing if we didn't shop, and wrap and decorate and rush around for the six weeks before Christmas, the family would essentially go without.

Putting up the Christmas lights and tree are the only real "guy" chores of the holiday season, and even at that, major negotiations are involved.

"Could you do it tomorrow before the guests come over?" "OK what about next week then?" I mean, why put up the lights when it's a balmy minus five, when you can wait until it's minus 25?

Same goes for the tree. In my house we have an artificial tree that needs to be carried up half assembled from the basement. That 30-second job done, my husband will agree to hang exactly one ornament before slinking off to his den. He will, however, feign delight when I call him out to view the final product.

Think about it. Who writes the Christmas cards? Women. Who wraps the family gifts? Women. Who bakes the Christmas cookies? Women.

Ok, to be honest, I'm a bit of a domestic dunce, so I don't actually bake, but my girlfriends spend hours making shortbread, tarts, squares and half a dozen other holiday treats. It's enough to make you slip an extra shot into your eggnog.

When men do venture out to shop it's usually with one person in mind, their significant other, and even at that they get a helping hand. I spend a day or two scouting out my own Christmas presents. Ah there's a nice sweater, I'll have them put it away so my husband can pick it up later. The watch? Tell him they need to remove three links when he picks it up so the bracelet fits.

6

Some stores even have special men's shopping nights complete with cigars and scotch served by pretty young ladies. The guys have a good time, buy a couple of gift certificates, and voila! half the work is done.

I'd like a special women's shopping night. We could soak our feet in pedicure basins, sipping on white wine while jazz plays softly in the background. Handsome young men would arrive showing off sample tools and ties, then wrap them while we enjoyed our holiday massages.

A couple of years ago my Mom ventured a wild and distressing proposal. What if we just stopped giving gifts to each other at Christmas? We'd still buy for the kids, but skip the hassle of drawing names and trying to find presents for each other. She figured birthdays were more important, so we'd save the gift buying for those special occasions.

Wow. I agreed somewhat reluctantly, but now I see the pure genius of her plan. It has reduced my Christmas stress level by about 40 per cent. Way to go Mom!

Despite my griping about the division of labour I do love Christmas. Shopping hassles aside, it's a warm and happy time of the year to reconnect with your loved ones.

It's also my birthday on Christmas Day, so that makes the 25th extra special. It also puts added pressure on my husband to double up on the gifts.

Even though I do a lot of the legwork, he always come through with a thoughtful little surprise or two that makes me realize just how well he knows and loves me. So I don't mind giving him a little help. (By the way, dear, I'd really like a digital camera this year for Christmas. The Canon A-70. There's a good deal on at…) ■

left to right - Lynda's husband Norm, and his older brother Steve

Flashlights And Satellite Radio

I'm feeling like a man these days — albeit an effeminate man.

Or maybe I'm feeling a bit like a woman who wishes, just for the month of December, that she were married to another woman.

Before you get your knickers in a knot, this is NOT a column about same-sex marriage; it's a last-minute lament about the gender divide when it comes to Christmas shopping.

I'm feeling like a guy, because for the first time in my adult life it looks like I'm going to wade into the testosterone-fuelled masses the week before Christmas, and do all my gift buying in one day.

I'm seriously bagged. After staff shortages at work, an intense television news ratings period, and the Tory leadership race, I'm left staring at my desk calendar in disbelief thinking, "It's the middle of December? What happened to November?"

I'm usually the queen of organization, the gifts bought and wrapped and under the tree by the first week of December. This year I barely got the tree out of storage. I usually place the lights just so, this year I stumbled round and round

6

the tree until the strings were strung, half-heartedly tossed on some ornaments and collapsed on the sofa. Good enough.

So I feel like a man because my stress load has turned me into a last-minute Christmas shopper. But I also feel like a woman who wishes her husband was a woman so I could shop with confidence, and get it over with in one afternoon.

Why are men so bloody hard to buy for?

I know my husband better than any other human being on the planet. But when it comes to Christmas shopping, I wrack my brains trying to find gifts that will surprise and delight, and usually come up short.

I remember seeing an old black and white photo of my husband as a tow-headed boy on Christmas morning. He was sitting round the tree in his flannel pyjamas with his brothers opening presents. The photo captured a perfect freeze frame of joy. Norm, triumphantly holding up a toy gun and holster set, his little boy cheeks stretched wide with a grin of pure delight. We've been together 20 years now, and I've yet to see that expression duplicated on Christmas morning. It's my life mission.

Problem is, if he really covets something, he'll go get it himself. He has very specific tastes, and if it's electronic, he wants to research the various products for weeks before making a decision.

He's been talking about satellite radio, but after scouring the Internet, the model he really wants is not available in Canada yet. He needs another watch, but he's extremely picky about the brand and appearance, so I'm not going to be able to surprise him on that front.

Do you see the hell you men put us through at Christmas time?

I was griping to my co-anchor Gord on the news set during a commercial break the other day... whining that women are so easy to please, get us anything — perfume, sweaters, costume jewelry, books, spa certificates, candles, etc. Guys like weird, obscure things like flashlights.

"Oh, flashlights!" Gord's eyes lit up. "I LOVE flashlights. Just talking about them is exciting."

Oh brother.

"I love pocket knives too," he enthused, "And combat knives, and swords."

It's official. Men really are from Mars. They can take their flashlights and knives to the red planet, while listening to satellite radio.

Me? I'm going to go lie on the couch for a while. ■

Lynda and husband Norm at the Global Christmas Party

What… This Old Thing?

I'm going to do something wild and crazy at this year's company Christmas party, something highly inappropriate and unconventional, that will raise eyebrows and have them gossiping in the bathroom. I'm going to wear the same dress I wore last year.

Oh I know what you're thinking. How gauche — how could she?

Well I don't care. I'm sick of spending money every year on a fancy dress that gets one, at best two, twirls around the dance floor before being relegated to the back of my closet, never to see the light of day again.

It's an expensive bit of business for one night of the year. You find the perfect cocktail dress, then you need to buy the right shoes, sheer nylons, strapless bra, earrings, necklace, maybe a new lipstick in the exact shade. After visiting

6

the hair salon for a Christmas up do, you've swiped your VISA to the tune of several hundred dollars.

Guys don't have this holiday pressure. On party night they open the closet, grab a jacket and tie, and they're good to go. I work with men who've worn the same tweed Tip Top blazer to the Christmas banquet since 1985. It's not fair.

I used to care more about my festive attire. I was born on December 25th, so for years my Mom bought me a Christmas cocktail dress for the office party as a birthday gift.

One year it was a spectacular black velvet affair. Open backed, and deep plunging in the front, the dress was held together with a simple crystal button at the base of the neck. The prearranged seating plan had us noshing at the boss's table, the late Dr. Charles Allard, an impressive — and to a young reporter — intimidating man.

I was seated for all of 30 seconds when the crystal button popped off, and rolled under the table behind us. I slapped my palm to my chest, just in time to prevent full frontal nudity. As my husband crawled around on the carpet looking under people's feet for my lost button, I had to walk across the hotel ballroom holding my limp dress to my chest looking for a needle and thread. Not my finest moment.

Maybe I'm sick of dressing up every day for work, or maybe I'm just getting old and cranky, but I don't have the same enthusiasm for getting gussied up for the company Christmas bash. I'd rather wear a comfy pair of jeans and sweater and sit in front of a roaring fire sipping a glass of white wine and chatting with colleagues I don't get a chance to spend much time with during the year.

I know I'm in the minority here. A straw poll of my female friends and colleagues revealed that most are quite excited about shopping for a new Christmas party frock. It's a fun excuse to buy something sparkly and new, and for many women, it's the only chance of the year to get really dressed up.

But would they dare to wear the same party dress to the same company function two years in a row? The survey says… emphatically NO.

One friend explained it this way: "I wouldn't want people snidely remarking, 'Didn't she wear that last year?' "

Well here's something interesting. Colleagues I polled on the subject admitted they had absolutely zero recollection of what I wore to the Christmas party last year. Couldn't remember the colour, style or length. Blank. Zip. Nada. No idea.

Aha! Here's my out.

"Really you don't recall? It was a long red dress. No wait, that was 2004. Last year I wore a short aquamarine halter dress. No hang on — it was a winter white pantsuit with pearls — yeah that's what it was. You really can't remember that?" Sweet.

I'm going to save myself a pile of time and money this year. ■

6

Christmas Correctness

Picture this: You're sitting in a wingback chair by the fireplace, a glass of spiced eggnog in hand, as the 12 Days of Holidays plays softly on the stereo.

Your husband is hanging the final ornament on the six-foot holiday tree you bought from the corner lot last week. It's a fine specimen this year, straight and full, with a pile of gaily-wrapped holiday gifts nestled round the base.

The children are snuggled into their pajamas, excited to watch The Grinch Who Stole the Holidays on TV.

Yes, the word Christmas is slowly and insidiously being erased from our collective consciousness.

A quick scan of the flyers in this week's newspaper had Canada Post trumpeting its "2005 Holiday Sending Guide". Rexall urging consumers to "Make the holiday MAGIC!" Office Depot offering up suggestions "For your Holiday Memories"... and the list goes on.

Wal-Mart encourages its staff to say "Happy Holidays" instead of "Merry Christmas".

The retail giant recently faced a consumer boycott in the States, after being accused of discriminating against Christmas, while promoting other seasonal holidays by names like Kwanzaa and Hanukkah.

Is it political correctness gone too far — or recognition and respect of other cultures and religious beliefs?

I did a straw poll at work recently.

One colleague said, "If Wal-Mart's action contributes in any way to the general recognition in our western culture that the face of our population is very different than it was 100 years ago, then I'm all for it."

Another said, "I don't really care if Wal-Mart or any other store wishes me anything. All I care is that their prices are low. My celebrations happen at home, not in aisle five."

Most people I polled are offended by the crass commercialism of it all...

suggesting Canadian retailers are more concerned about profits than actually offending anyone.

The great Christmas vs. Happy Holidays debate has also crept into our schools.

A colleague with two young children is frustrated that the Edmonton public school system has been calling it the 'holiday break'. Even the school's traditional Christmas tree has been renamed the 'holiday tree'.

An Edmonton government worker complains that her staff Christmas party has been renamed the "holiday party".

A friend's staff dinner was actually boycotted one year because it was labelled a "Christmas party". The shindig was rescheduled for February and called a "Festivus Celebration". Good grief.

It's a multi-faceted debate. For some it's all about religion.

One fellow I know is angry saying, "It's time Canada got a backbone and told all those politically correct interest groups that Canada is historically a Christian society, and you better live with it."

Another colleague who responded to my poll says, "The last time I looked, our constitution frowned on discrimination of religious practices, and that's EXACTLY what is happening with Christmas."

Some feel offended by society's attempt to "neuter" the meaning of Christmas.

"They've made it into a secular, grey kind of day," lamented one colleague.

"I don't want Ramadan's name changed or watered down, or Kwanzaa or Hanukkah… why change Christmas?"

Then there's the tricky little matter of sussing out who may or may not be offended by an innocent Christmas salutation.

Short of distributing lapel buttons with a NO CHRISTMAS red circle warning to those who don't celebrate the occasion, how on earth can you tell?

I think we could all do well by chilling out just a little.

For me, Christmas is about an attitude. It's about warmth and love and peace and goodwill toward your fellow man. A time to embrace family and friends — even total strangers.

If we're lucky, we get a few days away from the salt mines. Time to sit back and breathe, relax and reconnect with the people we love the most.

So whatever your position, whatever your faith, please don't take offence.

If I wish you a Merry Christmas, it means only that I sincerely hope you have a warm and wonderful time with your loved ones. ■

6

Miscellaneous Musings

Fighting The Good Fight

I'm a little freaked out right now.

My friend Trish is 38. She's beautiful, funny, intelligent, spunky, engaged-to-be married... and she's just been diagnosed with breast cancer.

"Over and over you ask, why me? Why now?" Trish admits.

"I couldn't say the words breast cancer without crying."

Trish is being incredibly brave and positive, but I'm furious. This crap disease is wreaking havoc on my extended Global News family.

You see, Trish is not just a friend, she's engaged to Dean Millard, Global Edmonton's weekend sports anchor.

"I was in a state of denial," Dean recalls, "thinking, wait a minute, this isn't happening again to someone so close to me."

Breast cancer has been a malevolent force in Dean's life. His mother Jean-Marie died at the age of 46 after cancer spread from her breast to her bones. Dean was just 19 when she passed away — a young man shattered by his mother's death.

Global meteorologist Nicola Crosbie can relate to Dean's personal heartache.

Her Mom Bridget was just 59 when she died from a lethal combination of breast and ovarian cancer. New research suggests a link between the two deadly diseases, so Nicola's been hyper vigilant ever since about monitoring changes in her own body.

She went for her first mammogram the other day.

"The technician really had to manoeuvre me into position," Nicola explains.

"Drop your arm here... relax your shoulder... tip your right hip forward... bend your left knee... she actually told me to swoon."

Nicola found it all rather amusing until the technician informed her the radiologist wanted a second set of X-rays.

7

"We're just a little concerned about this." The mild-mannered technician pointed to a white mass on the upper left breast.

So they did the mammogram dance again. More swooning, more manoeuvring.

The radiologist still wasn't happy. A third set of X-rays was ordered.

"Now I was really scared," Nicola confesses.

"I thought, oh my God, this is how it happens. I was thinking of all the women they see in this clinic who get the worst news of their life."

But Nicola was one of the lucky ones. A final check of the X-rays and she got the all clear. She left the clinic both relieved and deeply rattled.

Breast cancer has also thrown my co-anchor Gord Steinke for a loop.

He was devastated when his mom Donalda was diagnosed with a form of breast cancer called Paget's disease in 1999. It mimics the skin disorder eczema. By the time she had it looked at by a doctor, she needed a mastectomy.

"I tell women to do as I say, not as I did." Donalda warns, "Have any irregularities checked by a doctor immediately."

Gord's Mom is a survivor, who now works to raise money for, and awareness about, breast cancer in Saskatchewan. She even manages a dragon boat team made up of other breast cancer survivors. And she has a message of hope for others.

"Breast cancer is not a death sentence! Many women recover and lead normal, vibrant lives."

My friend Trish is in the most important battle of her life, and she's telling her story in hopes of educating, and maybe even saving another woman from going through her own personal hell.

"If there's anyone out there reading this article who doesn't know how to complete a breast self-examination, please ask," Trish pleads.

"Breast cancer is not a disease for women in their 50s anymore. Since I've been diagnosed, I've heard about a 21-year-old, a 28-year-old pregnant woman, I know of a 32-year-old. It's also a disease that men can get."

Trish, your Global Edmonton family is there for you all the way. And so, it seems, is a very special angel.

"I think my Mom is somehow watching over us right now, and guiding us through this." Dean quietly admits. "That may sound strange, but to me it's comforting."

Fight the good fight Trish and Dean. We love you both. ■

7

Laptop Diaries - Miscellaneous Musings

Lynda and long time friend Ross McLaughlin

I Am Canadian

Hockey, Tim Hortons coffee and universal health care.

Those are just a few of the things I like about Canada.

It's clean, safe, beautiful and affordable.

Canadians are seen as peacemakers, independent thinkers, polite and friendly. We're so likable some travellers are even pretending to "be" us these days.

A Mexico-based website called tshirtking.com is selling Canadian "disguises" online. They're kits designed to help Americans travelling overseas to avoid being hassled about U.S. foreign policy. For $24.95, you get a Canadian lapel pin, patch and T-shirt, plus a guide called How to Speak Canadian, Eh?

As Americans pose as Canadians abroad — some Canadians are posing as Americans here at home.

The U.S. retail giant Neiman Marcus has quietly taken over the entire upper floor of Westmount Mall.

7

As many as 700 Edmonton phone operators work during peak seasons, taking orders for everything from fashions to furniture.

Americans are protectionists. They hate the idea of a U.S. company hiring people in other countries to sell their merchandise, so the deception begins.

"You get a whole session on speaking Americanese," says Diane, a former employee who worked at the Neiman Marcus call centre last Christmas.

The operators are instructed to say "zee" instead of "zed."

"Don't say 'out and about' because right away they'll know you're from Canada."

If the customer wants to know where the call centre is located, the employees are encouraged to say: "Oh, we're just north of Dallas — next item, please!"

Diane says her first caller was an elderly woman with a thick Texas drawl.

"This old dolly said, 'Honey, I was born and brought up in Dallas, and you don't sound like nobody I've ever heard from around here.'

"And I said, 'Oh you smarty pants… I was born in Canada.' 'I knew it,' she said. 'I knew it! You sound just like my friend in Toronto!' "

Diane smiles… "It wasn't a lie. I was born in Canada."

My good friend Ross McLaughlin knows what it's like to make a living by posing as an American.

Ross was the original Troubleshooter consumer reporter for ITV in the early 1990s, when an American TV agent spotted his talent and moved him to Seattle.

At first, viewers harassed Ross about his Canadian pronunciation of words like "process" and "garage."

"When you move here, Americans want you to become a part of the American culture," Ross explained. "They left me voice mail saying 'You're American now — speak English, damn it!' "

Accent issues aside, Ross has had great professional success in the United States, moving from Seattle to L.A. to Washington, D.C.

Laptop Diaries - Miscellaneous Musings

After a decade of living south of the border, he says it's clear that "Canadians are a lot less accepting of Americans than Americans are of Canadians."

That sentiment echoes a famous quote from Canadian author and scholar John Bartlet Brebner, who once said: "Americans are benevolently ignorant about Canada, while Canadians are malevolently well-informed about the United States."

Ross thinks Canada's identity crisis may be to blame.

"The whole beer commercial thing with Molson, people standing up and cheering this anti-American sentiment that's been growing in Canada — the whole thing with the airspace, the missile treaty — Canada not being there when the U.S. went to war with Iraq. I think Canadians are trying to find their own identity by kicking out at the superpower."

I spent a long weekend with Ross in D.C. recently, where he told me he's somewhat reluctantly in the process of applying for his American citizenship.

"I go home and I get a sense of pride. I wish I could be in Canada, and live the life in Canada that I live here — the energy, the opportunities, the entrepreneurial spirit."

Just as I thought I'd lost my Canadian friend to the great U.S. of A., a sweet moment pulled us back to our roots.

We were spending our last afternoon together in the National Museum of American History.

As we rested on a bench in the civil war exhibit, I confessed to having trouble with the lyrics of O Canada. I know the words but sometimes get the lines mixed up.

Ross was horrified. He claimed to know the song by heart. I insisted he prove it.

So in the dimly lit Smithsonian, he softly sang me the Canadian anthem. Top to bottom, no hesitation.

He ended the song with a big smile and a hug.

The American advantage aside — apparently once a proud Canadian, always a proud Canadian. ■

Lynda's Arabian Adventure

It was an unforgettable introduction to the Middle East.

Standing on a rooftop at dawn with roosters shrieking in the distance and the air a muggy 25 C, I was startled by a hauntingly beautiful sound. The first call to prayer of the day was being played over loudspeakers mounted on dozens of mosque minaret towers.

My Arabian adventure had begun. And I was about to discover that being a white, western woman in the Middle East is an interesting, and slightly disconcerting experience.

My husband and I were visiting a friend from Edmonton who's teaching at a woman's college in Al Ain, a city about an hour's drive south of Dubai, in the emirate of Abu Dhabi.

Life there is an intriguing blend of old-world culture, and new-world commerce.

These people are wealthy. They get free education, free health care, cheap gas, and government subsidies. The Emirians have massive houses, maids and

7

cooks. They drive expensive, fast vehicles, and the women have a fondness for designer clothes.

On the surface it seems like a pretty cushy life. But the rules are very different here for men and women. For one thing, those designer duds are largely kept hidden.

While the men wear crisp, white dishdasha robes and head scarves in the searing desert heat, the women are cloaked head-to-toe in jet black robes called abeyyas.

They don't want to "tempt" strange men, so they cover their faces with black scarves called shaylas, peering out at the world through a two-inch slit.

Older, married women sometimes wear metallic looking face shields called burkas that cover their forehead, nose and mouth. The fabric comes from India, and leaves a purplish, black stain on their skin.

It was frankly tough not to stare. And they had trouble not staring back — at me — a white, blond woman from the West.

Despite the heat, I wanted to respect their culture, so I wore long sleeved t-shirts and pants. Yet I was still a curiosity, especially in the open-air marketplaces. At the camel souk, we drove quickly between the pens, trying not to draw attention to ourselves, but the Arab traders still gaped at the apparently bizarre sight of a Western woman riding in the back of an SUV.

At a local restaurant we were quickly ushered past the kitchen to the back forty of the eatery. My friend Wayne said, "You know we're sitting back here because of you." I guess female customers are bad for business.

But this is a land of contradictions.

While local women are shrouded and protected, the men think it's perfectly OK to head to the Rotana Hotel in Al Ain to ogle the belly dancer.

I was a bit perplexed to see this Brazilian beauty slink onto the dance floor in a turquoise, jewel-encrusted bra top and filmy skirt.

Given the conservative nature of the culture, how was this not offensive, I wondered aloud?

"It's not offensive, it's tolerable," smirked my dinner companion Mohammed, as he took a drag off his sheesha water pipe and turned his attention back to the dancer.

The men, it seems, have it made in the Middle East.

While their wives stay home in the evening, they're out socializing in the sand dunes.

It's common to see SUVs parked at the side of the road, with men sitting in circles around little bonfires chatting with their buddies.

The young women have to get permission from their brothers to go out. If they're married, their husbands make the decisions.

As an independent Canadian woman, this rankled me. I wondered, why do Arab women put up with it?

On a visit to the Al Ain Women's College, I had a chance to sit down with the 20 something students.

A few were interested in travelling, but most were perfectly happy with life in the Middle East.

They like the black abeyya gowns and head scarves — some even look forward to wearing a burka when they get married.

They feel safe, comfortable and privileged. They're OK with men making the decisions, that's just the way things are.

It was confusing.

If they don't feel oppressed, why do I feel sorry for them?

It was a fascinating educational experience, but I've never felt luckier to be a woman living in a country that embraces equal rights, and celebrates women's independence and achievements.

God bless Canada. It's good to be home. ■

7

Internet Dating

You never really know when - or where - you're going to meet the love of your life.

I was introduced to my husband twenty years ago during a police training exercise in the river valley. I was a rookie reporter - he was a dashing young tactical officer, with a handgun on his hip and a homemade bomb in his hand.

Next month we're going to celebrate our 18th wedding anniversary, and I still think he's a major catch.

Lets face it, a good marriage takes work, and it's not always rose petals and sunshine, but as the years go by, I'm more and more grateful "not" to be single. Dating after 40? No thanks.

I know some quality single women who are smart, funny and beautiful who simply cannot find a quality single guy over 40 who's not determined to date a woman under 30.

Many of these fabulous single women have resorted to that new millenium form of matchmaking. Internet dating. And while there may be some good guys online looking for love – you apparently have to kiss a swamp full of cyber toads to find a prince.

Call me old-fashioned… or just plain old - but online dating seems so impersonal. Or maybe imperfect is the right word. It's like cruising E-Bay looking for a used designer purse. It may look good in the photo, but is it really just a cheap fake?

I went to a wedding in Mexico a few years back, and one of the bridesmaids had brought along a guy she had met on the internet only weeks before. I was secretly shocked by that. Geez, do you really want to bring a guy you don't even know to your best friend's wedding… in a different country no less? What if he's a wingnut? What if he has bad hygiene? What if he's a serial killer who meets his victims online and then goes to weddings with them in Mexico? I mean really, how do you know?

Let's be honest. The internet is a place where liars often lurk behind phoney bios and lots of bravado. Yeah, yeah, I know there are decent guys online – but there's also a bunch of losers, fakes, paper tigers, druggies, and a whole lot of married men looking for a little sex-on-the-side.

After a bunch of my girlfriends had so-so or outright bad experiences, I was cynical, and frankly surprised to hear the internet dating scene is not always so bleak.

A friend of a friend – let's call her Lori – is a case in point. She's striking, fit, and eclectic. A creative, spiritual, intelligent creature who's been unlucky in love for years, and was recently goaded into posting her profile on a popular internet dating site called plentyoffish.com.

"I was really having a tough time wrapping my head around meeting 'him' online." Lori confesses.

She agreed to meet a few promising guys in person, but felt "angry and cheated" after they scored big online, but came up short in the flesh. That is, until Jack entered Lori's cyber universe. They spent no time chatting online, deciding to cut to the chase instead.

"No false ideals – no bull****," Lori explains, "Let's meet tonite for a beer, and see if we curl each other's toes and take it from there."

They met. He wasn't her physical ideal, but within 30 minutes they were smitten. After hours of long distance phone calls, and several weekend jaunts, "I'm packing to move to Alberta next week." Lori happily reports, "And although the independent, powerful urban woman fights the insinuation that it's for a guy... I'm scared, grateful, happy, excited... and in love."

Well shut my mouth. I guess you really "can" find love in the strangest of places.

I suppose the internet is no more unusual a meeting place than a police training exercise.

Way to go Lori and Jack. I hope you're lucky enough to celebrate your 18th wedding anniversary some day. ■

The Name Game

The day I met my husband, I was holding onto the tank of an old toilet as the doors exploded inward on an abandoned home in the river valley. When the smoke cleared, a tactical officer wearing a black balaclava was crouched at my feet pointing a handgun in my face.

It was an exciting television feature shoot and a dramatic introduction to the man I would marry. I had no idea that less than two years later I would be walking down the aisle with a handsome young police bomb technician, pondering life as Lynda Lipinski.

Don't get me wrong. Lipinski is a strong and proud Polish name — but aside from the obvious concerns about alliteration, it's just not me, if you know what I mean.

As a television journalist, I've spent years building my reputation, contacts and profile under the name Steele. It would be a challenge getting an interview with the mayor or premier if I called identifying myself as Lynda Lipinski. Who the heck is that?

Happily, my new husband didn't have a hangup about the surname issue, so it was a moot point when we married sixteen years ago.

The vast majority of my female friends and colleagues have also kept their maiden names, mostly for professional reasons. Take on a new surname mid-career and POOF! You cease to exist on e-mail. Your name's not in the phone book anymore. In the business world it's all about networking, and it's tough to maintain contact with someone who doesn't "officially" exist anymore.

Our birth names shape our identity, in some cases chart our destiny. A baby girl christened Hannah McLaughlin might well grow up to be a Supreme Court justice. Name your daughter Candi Storr and she could end up as a stripper.

Some women are saddled with unfortunate surnames they spend a lifetime trying to escape. A colleague grew up with a girl whose last name was Outhouse. She probably wasn't the prom queen in high school.

On the flip side, my friend has a distant relative named Hazel who married into the Knutt family. Now there's a case for keeping your maiden name.

But sticking with your birth name after marriage poses some challenges. What if you want to have children? "How come Mom doesn't have the same last name as me?" It's confusing for kids, and confusing for teachers who have to figure out who belongs to whom come report card time.

It's also a pain in the neck when it comes to bill payments. TELUS wouldn't give me a calling card recently because the phone is in my husband's name. It also refused to add my name saying it's against company policy to have two names on the bill. How aggravating.

I wonder what TELUS would do in Quebec? According to that province's civil code passed in 1981, it's actually against the law to take your husband's surname.

A woman is only allowed to use her husband's name for social reasons. No kidding.

After 50 years of marriage, my mom is still happy she took my dad's last name, but admits she wishes she'd given her maiden name Robson to my brothers and I as middle names. She says, "It would remind you that you're carrying the heritage of two families, rather than thinking of yourself only as a Steele." I know many women who've solved the maiden name dilemma by doing just that these days.

I also know of two men now in their late-fifties who took bold steps a few decades ago to resolve the surname debate. One agreed to hyphenate his name too, so both he and his wife could have the same last name. The other took it a step further. His wife was an only child and felt passionately about keeping the family name alive. In the end he agreed to give up his last name to take on hers. I'm impressed.

So there are creative solutions to the surname debate, but if you still chafe at the tradition of assuming a man's name upon marriage — consider this. You've already taken a man's surname. Your father's. ■

Lynda's husband Norm Lipinski doing police tactical training in downtown Edmonton

A Dangerous Day At The Office

When you marry a police officer, you marry into the extended law enforcement family.

I didn't know the 4 young RCMP officers gunned down in Mayerthorpe but my heart goes out to their loved ones and I think I speak for all police wives in Alberta.

My husband is a 25-year member of the Edmonton Police Service.

7

Over our 16-year marriage, he's dismantled bombs, interviewed children who've been sexually abused, fingerprinted bloated corpses and been harassed and attacked by drunks and druggies. He was even shot at once in the parking lot of an Edmonton shopping centre while chasing a fleeing bank robber.

A quarter-century of crime fighting… but never the ominous late-night knock on the door.

Thank God. I honestly can't imagine the grief. My friend Peggy Bevan can. She's the mother of a police officer, and the wife of a retired member of the Edmonton Police Service.

Her husband Dick was trying to arrest a bank robber holed up in an Edmonton apartment suite in the mid-1970s. He went into the washroom and pulled back the shower curtain to find the suspect crouched in the bathtub with a sawed-off rifle. Dick was shot through the elbow, and as he turned away from the blast the bullet went through his other arm as well. He was lucky to have survived.

Peggy says when she heard about the massacre in Mayerthorpe, "A terrible sadness washed right over me. It was personal for me, like this was my family. Unlike the tsunami disaster, this was personal…. I felt an obligation to grieve with them as both the mother of an officer and the wife of a policeman."

Along with sadness, many police families are feeling anger about the senselessness of the murders and the cowardice of the ambush.

Some police wives I know are angry with the justice system, saying the laws sometimes prevent their spouses from doing their jobs properly and safely.

There's also frustration directed at some members of the public who don't understand the tough job of policing and can't see past the uniform and badge to the human being underneath.

Think about it. Everyone loves firefighters. They're seen as yellow-clad heroes who hang off the sides of ladder trucks, sirens blaring, as they come to the rescue.

The police? We love them when we need them, when a child is lost or someone's broken into your house. We hate them when we get caught speeding or blowing through a red light.

My friend Franca is married to an EPS detective who works in West Edmonton. She says, "It just goes to show that we always bitch about police officers when things are not going our way. But they are the first ones we want there when things are going wrong… and I don't think people get that. Police officers throw their own safety to the wind to save complete strangers. How many other people would be willing to do that?"

Franca wonders if the tragedy in Mayerthorpe will make the public more appreciative of the tough work police officers are asked to do and the danger they're asked to put themselves in to protect their communities.

Unfortunately, that danger seems to be growing. There's even more violence these days and less respect for police.

Peggy Bevan says, "As the mother of a policeman it's a continual worry. I pray every night — pray that nothing happens to him — that I go first. I think there's so much more danger because of the artillery that's out there now. It seems there's less law and order; more gang activity and more brazenness. So that worries me even more."

As the wife or relative of a police officer you intellectually understand the risks but emotionally are never prepared for the worst.

My deepest condolences go out to the officers' loved ones. I cannot even imagine the magnitude of your grief. ■

7

The late Alberta Lieutenant Governor Lois Hole Photo: Akemi Matsubuchi

A Woman To Be Admired

This is a tribute to a great Albertan.

The news that Lois Hole had lost her battle with cancer made me very sad. But my sadness is tinged with gratitude for having seen a personal side to this very public woman.

I never knew quite what to call Lois Hole. Protocol dictated formalities like "Your Honour" which seemed a fussy handle for such a down-to-earth human being. This woman deserved respect and recognition, yet shrugged it off to embrace you with a bear hug instead.

That's what I liked most about Lois Hole. She was real.

She held one of the most prestigious offices in all of Alberta — and the ubiquitous black dress and pearls aside, she was never pompous. Far from it.

I played the ponies with the lieutenant-governor a couple of times at her brother-in-law Harry's annual get-together at Northlands. Let me tell you, that woman was either extremely lucky, or much better versed in the strategy of horse racing than I. She took great delight in studying the day's race book, then watching her educated hunches pay off at the cashier's wicket. We're talking hundreds of dollars here.

Lois Hole also liked red wine, and I had the pleasure of tipping a glass or two with her at various charity events over the years. We even shared a table with James Bond himself one night — the ever elegant Roger Moore.

007 regaled us with Hollywood tales, and while passing on the bun basket, confessed to a bizarre weight loss strategy. Moore said he'd been hypnotized to think bread (his main vice) tasted like coriander (an herb he detested). Mrs. Hole was most intrigued. Did it work? Had he lost weight? Did the bun "really" taste like coriander? (Yes, yes and yes).

The gala dinner with Moore was a UNICEF fundraiser. Retired Eskimo greats were serving as celebrity wine stewards, and I'm pretty sure our table was getting "topped" up more often than others.

So feeling the buzz, and the thrill of such inspiring dinner companions, I leaned over to Lois Hole and told her something I'd felt for a long time, but been too shy to actually voice.

I said: "I think you're the best lieutenant governor we've ever had. You're smart; you care; you're tireless; and you really connect with the people of Alberta."

This amazing woman got quiet for a moment and stared into her lap. I had a flash of angst, thinking I'd overstepped my boundaries, when Lois Hole looked up at me and said a quiet "Thank you."

I realized in that instant how seriously she took her responsibility as the Queen's representative in Alberta. How genuinely grateful she was to be recognized for doing a good job.

That "job" helped Lois Hole survive a great personal tragedy in 2003.

When her husband Ted passed away that spring, she ramped up her already hectic personal appearance schedule. Mrs. Hole's ever present companion Mountie Moe Wolff said she was lonesome, and felt buoyed by the caring and concern of regular Albertans.

Lois Hole loved her family, and she loved the land… her passion for plants never waning despite the onerous public schedule. She cheerfully offered advice on my sickly black ash last year — and counselled my co-anchor Gord on how to prune his backyard maples. This powerful woman loved a good ol' gab about gardening, and was always delighted to autograph one of her many bestselling books.

You see, books were very important to Lois Hole. A tireless champion of literacy projects — we crossed paths at many Edmonton schools over the years.

Without fail, the children shrieked with delight to see their de facto grandma arrive. She always shared an animated story — all raised eyebrows, booming voice and big sweeping gestures. The children were enchanted. We all were.

I distinctly remember my first Lois Hole hug. As a journalist, it was frankly a bit startling to be pulled into the lieutenant governor's embrace. A government representative hugging a member of the media? In public no less? It just wasn't done.

I'm going to miss my hugs from Lois Hole. She was a great Albertan. One of the best. ■

7

Laptop Diaries - Miscellaneous Musings

Roll Up The Rim

Road rage in the Tim Hortons drive-thru. Sound silly?

Take it from me. Never get between a cranky oil worker and his daily caffeine fix.

It was a normal weekday morning that quickly turned into a Mexican standoff with a burly blond guy in a white Ford F-150.

We were facing each other with blinkers flashing, both trying to join up with the tail-end of the drive-thru lineup.

Since I was there first, I edged forward with a smile and a wave, and was startled when my trucker friend laid on the horn and flailed his arms, spittle flying, apparently incensed that I was "cutting him off".

The guy was obviously a nut, so with a grandiose arm sweep, I invited the big man to go first. He graciously waved back with both middle fingers.

I've since discovered that road rage is not uncommon in the Tim Hortons parking lot.

Google the subject and you'll find all kinds of references to bumper bashing and screaming fits at Canada's favourite doughnut shop.

They may be hostile, but at least most customers keep their pants on.

An Ontario man was busted last fall, for carrying out a foolish fantasy. The guy made an early-morning run through a Tim Hortons drive-thru in the nude — and let's just say he only had one hand on the wheel.

When police caught up with him he reportedly admitted to doing "a bad thing", saying "fantasy" got the best of him.

That must have had Tim Horton rolling over in his grave.

Next month will mark the 32nd anniversary of the chain founder's death.

The NHL player and inventor of the apple fritter was racing his sports car home after playing a Buffalo Sabres game in Toronto in 1974. He was going 160 kilometres an hour when he crashed near St. Catharines and died at the age of 44.

At the time, there were 40 Tim Hortons stores. By December of 2005, there were 2,529 outlets in Canada, supplanting McDonalds as the largest fast food operator in the country.

There's no denying it. Canadians have fallen in love with Tim Hortons.

One customer even took his undying affection for the chain to his grave.

His will stipulated that the funeral cortege was to go through a Tim Hortons drive-thru, and all members of the funeral party were to have a cup of coffee on him.

Even Jesus made an appearance at Tim Hortons in 1988, his image appearing on the exterior brick wall of an outlet in Cape Breton. The reporter who chronicled this unexplained apparition for Saturday Night magazine dryly observed that "No one questioned the Son of God's choice of venue. Where else in Canada would Christ appear but at Tim Hortons?"

And where else but in Canada, would a coffee earn the nickname of "Gretzky"?

At Tim Hortons, that's code for 9 creams and 9 sugars. Get it? 99. The Great One's jersey number. No wonder Canadians are so fat.

Sugary doughnuts and full fat cream aside, Tim Hortons apparently does care about our health.

In 1983 it voluntarily opened its first non-smoking outlet, a controversial move well ahead of its time.

At first, smokers were incensed and refused to obey the rules, forcing staff to call police.

And that brings us full circle to the aggression that Tim Hortons seems to inspire in so many of its customers.

Sure, you get your daily dose of impatient, caffeine-deprived Canadians who bark at the overworked, and in my opinion, underpaid men and women who sport the beige "career wear". But I've also been the recipient of a random act of kindness at Tim Hortons.

After pulling up to the drive-thru window to pay for my large coffee, double cream, the worker waved me off, saying the driver ahead had already paid my tab in an anonymous gesture of goodwill.

Infinitely nicer than a middle finger salute, eh? ■

Hot Economy, Tepid Service

If you've experienced lousy customer service in the past month, raise your right hand.

Welcome to the disgruntled consumer's club of Alberta.

According to the web site dictionary.com, the definition of customer service is:

"Assistance and other resources that a company provides to the people who buy or use its products or services."

Well I'm not getting much assistance these days, and I know I'm not alone.

I tried to buy a pair of running shoes the other day. The store was busy - the staff looked harried and unhappy, so I stood patiently with shoe in hand waiting my turn.

After 5 minutes of being completely ignored, I was forced to approach an employee myself and ask to try on the runner in question. The young man saw the brand, snorted, said, "We don't have any," and walked away. I asked his back if they were getting any in soon, and he told me to go to a competitor instead. I did. Thanks for nothing pal.

At a major hardware store, the wooden patio set I wanted was in a large flat box on a chest high dusty shelf. Two middle aged male employees stood by and watched as I struggled to drag the heavy box off the shelf and onto the top of a shopping cart by myself. They never once offered to help. Bad service is one thing, but what ever happened to simple good manners?

When I made an appointment with a medical specialist recently, I was told it was up to "me" to call the day before to confirm I was coming, or the appointment would be cancelled.

Then there's the not-so-fast food industry. I love Tim Hortons coffee, but I've finally given up on the franchise. I waited so long in the drive-through the other day, a panhandler actually walked up and knocked on my window asking for change.

It must be very frustrating to run a small business these days. With thousands of people moving here to cash in on the Alberta advantage, the help wanted signs are everywhere, but not enough people are willing or able to make a go of it on minimum wage.

7

A Red deer restaurant actually posted a sign on the front door this summer, apologizing in advance for the bad service it's customers were about to receive, explaining it was experiencing major staff shortages.

I do have sympathy for the overworked and often underpaid employees, especially in the food industry. They take the brunt of the abuse from frustrated customers, but they also know they hold the trump card these days.

I heard a crazy story recently about a bartender at a busy Edmonton restaurant.

He was given last minute free tickets for a concert on a Friday night. When the boss said he couldn't go because they were short-staffed, the bartender allegedly quit on the spot.

As he walked out the door, he smiled at his co-workers and said "See you tomorrow!" knowing he wouldn't be fired, because the boss needed him too badly.

What kind of message does that send the young workers of today? That they can get away with surly, lackluster behaviour on the job with impunity? Great. Where does that leave the rest of us? Surely the Better Business Bureau is being flooded with complaints?

Amazingly not. The BBB says the number of customer service complaints in Edmonton is holding steady at about 20 a month – same as last year. Most are about delayed response times, slow and inadequate service.

The bureau's operation's manager, Jodi Doesburg, is hearing from customers frustrated by restaurant and storeowners who say, "If you don't like my service, the next person will. I don't need your business."

Well I have a word of advice for those blasé shopkeepers cashing in on the hot economy, with little regard for customer satisfaction. Remember the recession in the early 1980's?

Good service breeds customer loyalty that will keep them coming back when you need their business the most. ■

The Professor Of Purse Trivia

Two tampons, six packets of Splenda, cell phone, day timer, wallet, digital tape recorder, makeup bag, pen, nail file, sunglasses.

There you have it. My life tucked inside a black faux alligator Nine West handbag.

It's 99 per cent organized (one per cent chaos) — a reflection of my life, according to Sandra LeBlanc, the professor of purse trivia.

"A messy handbag equals a messy mind."

The Edmonton mother of three has just successfully defended her thesis for a masters of arts at the U of A, majoring in sociology. Subject? The history of the handbag, and the role purses play in society today.

Sound frivolous? Try fascinating.

Let's start with the power purse. The five thousand dollar Hermes handbag — or Judith Leiber one-of-a-kind evening clutch.

"It's the equivalent to a man driving a power car... a Ferrari kind of thing." LeBlanc explains, "It says I have copious amounts of money, and I want you to know about it."

That kind of purse pomposity got Martha Stewart in trouble with the tabloids during her recent trial for insider trading. She was regularly photographed going into court carrying a ten thousand dollar Birkin handbag.

LeBlanc says Stewart's critics felt she was thumbing her nose at the rest of the world. "I am a rich, powerful, successful woman and therefore I am above the law. She took a lot of heat for that."

If you'd rather run down Jasper Avenue in your underwear than spend ten thousand dollars on a purse — LeBlanc says you may be a "Sears handbag" kind of gal. More department store than designer. Someone who cares less about fashion, and more about whether the bag has enough compartments for all her stuff.

The briefcase signifies a professional woman — In control, educated, dependable, responsible.

7

Backpack screams student. It's all about convenience, utility.

Diaper bag? New mom. You've got the wet wipes, baby bottle, might as well throw the wallet in there too.

Regardless of your purse personality, Sandra LeBlanc says all women have one thing in common. We care about the contents of our handbag. We're deeply afraid of having it lost or stolen.

"I don't know how many women said to me, 'my life is in my purse', because women carry a driver's licence, credit cards, some even carry their passports. There's that whole element of vulnerability — you're carrying a lot of important stuff around."

Important stuff like guns. During her research in Nashville, LeBlanc found many American women carry small handguns in their bags. In Edmonton, several women confessed to carrying mace.

No wonder Sigmund Freud was freaked out about the female purse.

Freud had some pretty strange theories, like Vagina dentata. Translation: toothed vagina. It speaks to Freud's fear of women castrating men during intercourse.

What's the connection to purses you ask?

"Freud, he was really kind of afraid of the purse." LeBlanc explains. "He saw it as having a pink, silky interior… something that was dark and secretive… you don't really know what's in there."

LeBlanc concedes some modern day men may actually share Freud's fear of the purse — for very different reasons.

"It's kind of a holder of secrets. Young girls will carry birth control or condoms, cigarettes or drugs. Some women even carry their diaries… and potentially incriminating things like a lover's letter. I think that really lends this aura of mysteriousness to the interior of the purse."

Think about it. Ask a man to get you something out of your purse, and he'll hand you the bag and tell you to get it yourself.

I'm not sure what their problem is. Men were the first to carry purses hundreds of years ago. Little handbags containing orange scented potpourri, flint and money. In 1670, breeches with built-in pockets came into vogue, and men didn't need to carry purses anymore.

Today, men tote their personal stuff around in briefcases, messenger bags or fanny packs. Call it what you will - just don't call it a purse.

"For most men, that's a feminine word," Sandra laughs, "and they really, really do not want to be associated with anything feminine. That's a social taboo for men."

Not all guys are deterred though. Some new millenium men are flaunting their high fashion handbags — the critics be damned.

I'm pretty liberal, but when it comes to purses, there's something... well... wrong about a man carrying a purse.

Really guys, what would Freud think? Leave the pink silk and mystery to the ladies. ■

7

Lynda on the beach in Maui

Beach Diary

Ever try on a bikini in February? It's a humbling experience.

Pasty white skin displayed in three-way splendor — every bump and jiggle, pucker and roll reflected back in the harsh reality of overhead fluorescent bulbs.

A recent Hawaiian vacation got me thinking about the body beautiful.

Is anyone 100-per-cent happy with the skin they were born in? I hit the beach with notebook in hand looking for the answer.

Maui Beach Diary Day One

- 8:45 a.m.

> Cross paths with sexy septuagenarian on sunrise beach jog... Jack LaLanne fitness type — barrel chest, trim waist. Pecs saluting sand, but guy's still a dandy: longish white hair swept back, deep tan, half-dozen faded tattoos. Former Navy Seal? Rebel biker? Ex-con? Physically captivating in way not usually associated with senior citizens. Rock on mystery man.

- 11:30 a.m.

Mid-50s lady lounges near resort gates — blinding fuschia and turquoise one-piece, cut low across bum like '50s pin-up. Colourful bathing suit sets off enormous and oddly disturbing nest of copper hair perched atop head (surely a wig?). Spry and thin bathing beauty marches with confidence to beach, alone, yet not lonely.

- 1 p.m.

Heat forces move to shade of banyan tree... Me: 40-something Canadian, white tankini, flushed face, pulsing sandal blisters, itchy leg rash from snorkling excursion, humidity hair (think Streisand in Meet the Fockers).

Her: 40-something Asian woman wearing opaque silver tights, suede ankle boots, short shorts, bedazzled jean jacket with upturned collar, movie-star sunglasses and Louis Vuitton handbag... (One of us looks like a kook. You decide.)

- 2:15 p.m.

Floating frat party passes surfside burger bar — beautiful young bodies tumbled atop six neon rafts lashed together. Rogue air mattress cuts for shore prompting chubby girl on beach to attempt rescue mission. Cheerful volunteer fights through surf out to party raft to deliver mattress, but efforts ignored by self-indulgent cool kids. Heavyset girl trudges back to beach and waves slow goodbye to "new friends" who pay zero attention.

Beach Diary Day two —

Waikiki, Honolulu

- 11:15 a.m.

Different beach — new cast of characters. One-handed European heavyweight squats in eye-popping lime green thong, ignores posted warnings about stinging jellyfish and wades into ocean. (Micro suit proves more shocking upon frontal view). Balding beach boy checks flaxen locks in portable vanity mirror, lights smoke and rolls on to back to intensify sunburn. Later spotted pulling Houdini-like switcheroo from thong to white industrial-sized gaunch. Appalling lack of modesty? Or admirable lack of self conciousness? Jury's out...

- 11:40 a.m.

Two pretty Asian teens in striped bikinis frolic in surf — snapping model style photos with digital camera phones (never seen so many "plugged-in" people on the beach before). Girls seem more fascinated by technology than natural surroundings. Hour later — teens pack up and move on to next photo friendly location.

- 1:25 p.m.

Late 30's blond wearing two-piece athletic swimsuit, good physique, bad body image. Takes step — adjusts crotch of suit — takes step — picks at elastic along bum — step — adjust waistband — step — check crotch line — step — adjust bra top. Step — pick — step — pick... obsess — obsess — obsess! Alone, anonymous and utterly self-concious.

- 2:40 p.m.

Manic toddler leaps and twirls with excitement, thrilled to be on beach vacation with parents, runs into surf wearing neon orange inflatable ring, slaps joyfully at water, chases little brother through sand, then swings from young Mom's arm 'til shorts fall down to ankles.

With that sweet and amusing moment, my covert beach research was complete.

When it comes to accepting our physical flaws, it seems the very young are blissfully unaware of body image and the very old just don't care anymore. It's all us "inbetween age" folks that can't stop obsessing about the body beautiful.

How sad. ■

7

Gord & Lynda make good on a bet with their North Carolina TV colleagues

I Bet You Fifty Bucks...

The problem with betting is, you actually have to make good when you lose, and I hate losing.

So why do I make these silly wagers? It seems like a fun and spontaneous thing to do at the time - a low risk way to put your personal convictions on the line.

My colleagues bet on just about anything. Who's going to win the election, and by how many seats? Who's going to come out on top in this year's edition of the reality TV show Rock Star?

I recently bet a co-worker five bucks that injured Oilers goalie Dwayne Roloson would be back in net before the end of the playoffs. He actually felt bad taking my cash.

"Not only do the Oilers lose, but you owe me money too."

I also made a cross border bet with the NBC anchors in Raleigh, North Carolina.

The deal was, if the Oilers won, my co-anchor Gord and I would fly to Raleigh and anchor part of the NBC newscast while mercilessly taunting our American colleagues decked out in Oilers gear.

If Carolina won, Gord and I would have to wear Cane's jerseys on the anchor desk and produce a story about how great our rivals are both on and off the ice.

Do you know how hard it is to find a couple of Hurricane's jerseys in Edmonton? Bloody hell.

Thank god I'm not a real gambler. When I make a bet, the stakes are never higher than five bucks or a steaming plate of crow for dinner.

Casinos bore me, and even Vegas holds limited interest. I was half-heartedly playing a nickel slot once when coins began clattering into the metal collection tray. My heart rate shot up, and as I frantically looked around for my husband, the woman on the stool next to me took a drag off her cigarette and said,

"Ain't it just like a man to walk away the second you hit the jackpot?"

The thrill of winning $40 dollars worth of nickels quickly dissipated. We traded our bucket of coins for tickets to a cabaret show.

But it got me to thinking. Why are some people able to gamble a little and walk away, while others are totally consumed by it?

'There could be a genetic factor, it could be brain chemistry, a learned behaviour, each contribute a little bit."

Professor Garry Smith is an expert in gambling addictions at the University of Alberta.

He says the social gambler does it occasionally, spending only what they can afford. Infrequent gamblers buy the odd lottery ticket. Frequent gamblers play a skill game like poker once or twice a week, but stay within their limits. At-risk gamblers are preoccupied with betting, wagering more than they should, and problem gamblers have an inability to control the situation. They set limits but always exceed them, and neglect important things in life, like remembering their child's birthday.

"They're not bad people, they just get overwhelmed by their addiction."

And that addiction can be devastating. Alcohol can hurt you, but after so many drinks, you pass out. A gambler can lose 100 thousand dollars and still be standing.

Professor Smith says problem gamblers are usually depressed, emotionally distant people who think about gambling all the time and often sacrifice their relationships to their addiction.

For most of us though, gambling is a relatively harmless way to have fun, bond with others, and fantasize about winning the big one. Who hasn't wasted a little time dreaming about how they'd spend a lottery jackpot? Buying a couple of lotto tickets a month is no big deal, but Professor Smith says the warning bells should go off if you or someone you love is buying 100's of tickets a month.

"Gambling is not a bad thing if you can control it."

Happily, I fall into the social gambler category. I put my loonies into the hat during office pools, buy the occasional scratch and win ticket, and make silly bets that don't cost much… except my pride maybe.

(Five bucks says the Eskimos make it to the Grey Cup this year.) ■

Shall We Dance?

I don't care much for ballroom dancing, but I'm fascinated by these reality dance shows on TV.

I marvelled at Heather Mills' ability to do the cha-cha on a prosthetic leg with synthetic toenails painted to match her fuschia ball gown. Even trash TV host Jerry Springer was entertaining on last season's Dancing with the Stars show, shaking his 60-something booty. I admire their enthusiasm, their chutzpah. You can tell they're having a blast out there, and it makes me feel a little wistful.

I used to love dancing too. I was never very good at it — but in my teens and early twenties, I would leap onto the dance floor at the slightest provocation. In my hometown of Hinton, I was often first up on the hardwood at the Athabasca Hotel bar. I liked getting the party started, and if that meant dancing in a circle with your girlfriends to encourage the guys to join in — so be it.

On one particularly memorable night, I cajoled a friend named Percy into an early start on the dance floor. Despite the ribbing of pals, he slammed back a glass of liquid courage, and ran enthusiastically toward the stage, vaulting himself cartwheel style over the metal railing that separated the dance floor from the bar tables. As the crowd roared, Percy staggered forward a few steps, then lurched sideways toward the men's washroom, face buried in his hands.

At first I thought he was kidding around — then I saw the blood streaming down between his fingertips. My would-be dance partner had slammed his forehead into the metal railing, opening a two-inch gash that required stitches. He never danced with me again.

As the years went by, something strange happened. My desire to dance began to wane. I really don't know why. I guess I started to feel... I don't know... self-consious? Less inclined to look silly? Less energetic? Who knows? Now only classic tunes like Brick House or Mustang Sally can get me up on the dance floor.

Good thing I married a guy who's not keen on dancing either. Our less than impressive dancing skills were put to the test the day we got engaged.

It was a champagne-fuelled affair in the mountains. We rented a canoe and were in the middle of Two Jack Lake in Banff when Norm proposed. We were both so exhilarated, we drank a ridiculous amount of bubbly, and then rushed to get ready for a celebratory dinner with my soon-to-be brother-and sister-in-law.

Giddy, and somewhat wobbly, we were ushered into the grand Rob Roy dining hall at the Banff Springs Hotel, where a live 40s-style swing band was entertaining the guests. Once we were seated, the conductor picked up the microphone, and to my horror announced to the crowd, "We've got a young couple in the house tonight that just got engaged, and we'd like to play a special song for them. Would you please welcome Norm and Lynda to the dance floor!" Aggggh.

After stumbling around in front of a ballroom full of strangers, we decided to take a few dance lessons so we wouldn't have a repeat performance on our wedding day.

We learned how to do a passable box step for the first dance, and I think we pulled it off all right, but 18 years later, I could count on my hands the number of times we've waltzed in public and still have a few fingers left.

I'm OK with sitting it out, but I do get a kick out of watching other people wind it up on the dance floor — especially if they can't dance, and don't care what other people think. It's joyful and uninhibited, and it takes me back to a more carefree time in my life, when things just didn't seem that complicated.

Maybe when I'm 70 I'll learn how to do the cha-cha. ■

Fly With Me

They used to be called "cart tarts" or "trolley dollys".

Remember when stewardesses were beautiful young women in short skirts and high heels, with bouffant hair and false eyelashes?

The in-flight meals were served on white linen with real cutlery and silver tea service.

Flash forward to 2005, and you're lucky to get a nuclear hot bunwich with your $500 plane ticket.

And the new millennium flight attendants? If you like knock-knock jokes, you'll love the perpetually chirpy staff at WestJet.

"Listen up folks! Who wants to hear Captain Dave sing 99 Bottles of Beer on the Wall?" (Uh - not me).

If you want your elbow fractured by a stern sky matron with a high-speed meal cart — try another airline.

Ever notice how some senior flight attendants seem to be actually annoyed by your presence? Why is that?

Maybe it's because these airline veterans have seen it all… from the sexually charged "Fly Me" ad campaign of the 1970s to the air paranoia post 9/11.

Frankly, I never gave much thought to the plight of the flight attendant until I was asked to narrate documentary for U.S. cable station History Television.

I didn't know the profession began in the 1930s with a feisty young nurse from San Francisco named Ellen Church.

Ellen was passionate about aviation — she even trained to become a pilot.

When no one would hire her, she convinced an airline executive he needed onboard nurses to make his passengers feel more secure. So Ellen recruited some nursing pals who became known as the Original Eight.

The era of the stewardess was born.

7

The flying nurses did things like serve meals and check the floor bolts — sometimes they even started the engines. In short order, there were nearly 300 nurses flying the friendly skies. But their role changed dramatically after the Second World War.

That's when commercial air travel really took off. By the early 1950s there were thousands of young women signing up for a glamorous career that promised travel to exotic locales.

The increased competition had airline executives more concerned about how their stewardesses "looked".

The women had to be over five-foot-two. Weight was strictly monitored. If you failed the regular weigh-in you were yanked from the flight. New recruits couldn't be married and once they hit the ripe old age of 32, they were fired.

Global TV's Fringe theatre reviewer Judy Unwin worked for Wardair in the mid-1960s.

Air travellers were pretty cheeky in that era.

Judy says "One time I was serving coffee to a passenger in the window seat, when a guy in the aisle seat reached up and grabbed my boobs." She responded by pouring scalding hot coffee in the randy passenger's lap.

The Wardair stewardesses were so used to being hit on, Judy says they memorized the phone number for Alberta Pest Control.

"People figured stewardesses were easy... so if someone was bugging you, trying to date you — we'd say here's my number!"

The women loved their globe-trotting jobs and the camaraderie, but they were sick of being treated like sex objects. So Pan Am stewardess Patricia Ireland helped kick-start a revolution.

Ireland refused to wear a girdle in flight — arguing the constricting garment was a health hazard at high altitude.

She went on to become president of the National Organization of Women.

The stewardesses marched on Washington and organized a group called Stewardesses for Women's Rights.

They demanded respect… and they got it in 1971, courtesy of a hijacker on board a 727 taking off from Oklahoma City. He was a mentally disturbed man with no political agenda, who eventually gave himself up on the tarmac.

For the first time, the flying public saw the stewardess, now called flight attendant, in a whole new light.

Passengers realized these people were not just handing out peanuts. They were trained safety professionals, and they had a potentially dangerous job to do.

If you ever doubted it, September 11th put those doubts to rest.

Cherylanne Dixon is a young flight attendant from Calgary who works for WestJet.

She says, "People are taking flying quite seriously now since September 11th. The sense of awareness is a lot higher… the idea that anything can happen."

From cart tart — to first line of defence.

Customer service is still a priority, but Cherylanne says these days, "Safety is the number one thing, it's the biggest part of the job."

So the next time you fly — even if you are getting lousy service — try to be nice to your flight attendants. They could save your life someday. ■

7

Lynda takes up the rear with guide Cody on the Kananaskis River

Taking A Risk

Have you ever voluntarily done something that might lead to your death?

Think about it. We're all risk takers on some level, and you can probably recall a time or two when you did something incredibly foolish that could have had deadly consequences.

I remember the exact instant I leapt out of a plane at 35 hundred feet. I was standing on the wing strut, heart racing, when the instructor yelled JUMP!

I pushed off, and immediately thought, "Well I hope you're happy, you've gone and killed yourself you damn fool."

Despite a moment of terror when my parachute lines were tangled, I survived, albeit with a twisted knee from a rocky landing.

My brother-in-law Eugene has been trying to kill me for years.

There was the time he led us on a hike to the Stanley Glacier in Banff.

7

When we arrived in the parking lot, there was a handwritten note held down by a rock that warned "Grizzly seen in area 07/23/05." I'm thinking to myself, geez that was yesterday – surely we're not still going? Uh yes, we are apparently. I was nervous for the first hour or so – on high alert for signs of a big bear. But after a picnic in the bowl of the glacier, and a quick snooze, I forgot all about the danger. That is until we met the monster on the way down. My brother-in-law hissed "there's the bear!" I caught a glimpse of its gigantic silvery brown head through the bushes. My first thought was "Cool!" My second thought was "Run!"

That was a stupid and unnecessary risk to take, but not quite as stupid as a champagne canoe trip down the raging Bow River many years ago. One photo shows Eugene and his wife smiling and holding up a champagne glass as they cruised by - the next photo shows my husband Norm and I soaked and stranded on the riverbank after hitting a logjam and dumping our canoe. Dumb.

Dumber yet was reprising the fateful canoe trip ten years later. This time no booze, but a faster more dangerous river. My brother-in-law took a right fork in the Bow, but the powerful current dragged my husband and I left, and – CRASH – we hit another massive logjam, the canoe tipped, and this time we were both sucked underneath a churning, glacially cold mass of whitewater. I remember feeling my expensive sunglasses leave my face as I flipped and tumbled under the logjam. My first thought was "ok you dumb a**, you've REALLY gone and killed yourself this time."

It was the closest call yet. We survived, but the borrowed birch bark canoe got sucked under the logjam and stayed there. We sheepishly paid the canoe's owner one thousand dollars and vowed never to hit the Bow again.

So when I suggested a white water rafting trip for my 12th annual girl's weekend, my friend Sue emailed to say "Aren't you the woman with a record for falling out of things on the river?"

The ladies wanted to go on a more sedate "float" instead. Turns out the float option wasn't available on the weekend, so we booked a Kananaskis rafting trip instead with modest 1 to 3 level rapids.

It was 34 degrees as we zipped up wetsuits and buckled on life jackets and plastic helmets. We piled into a raft filled with Pfizer drug reps from Atlanta, Georgia, and a guide named Cody who used to be a professional kayaker.

The river was dammed and manipulated to create a specific level of excitement. Here comes the first rapid...WOO HOO! Here comes another one...YES! Bring on the big boy rapids! What? That's it? Come on...that's as big as they get? Bummer. Even the most timid of my girlfriends was mildly disappointed.

Well I hope you're happy you granny panties.

Next year it's bungee jumping off a bridge in Whistler, BC - a 160 foot drop to the Cheakamus River below. Anyone game? ■

7

Soap Addicts

Hi my name is Lynda, and I'm an addict.

By day I'm a professional broadcaster. By night I indulge in my secret vice.

Soap operas.

Well, one soap opera to be exact — The Young and the Restless.

It's like a paperback novel that never ends. The storyline's not always great, but good enough to keep you turning the pages to see what happens next.

I've been watching the Y and R for a quarter century now, so I was intrigued when a cast member was in Edmonton last summer for the Grand Prix. David Shark Fralick plays an ex-con named Larry Warton on the daytime drama. It's a bit part at best, but Fralick was acting every inch the Hollywood star, cruising around town in a white stretch limousine — shades on, Von Dutch ball cap torqued to the side.

It took a little ego massaging, but after he dropped the TV star schtick, the L.A. actor had some interesting insights about the fascination fans have with the soaps.

"They can relate to it — sympathize you know. It's bringing up real life issues… like single mothers, rape victims, cancer, homelessness and stuff like that."

It was actually my second brush with soap stardom in the past year.

Last spring I met a couple of long time actors from Days of Our Lives in town to promote the opening of a new Edmonton spa.

Bill Hayes and his wife Susan Seaforth-Hayes play married couple Doug and Julie Williams on the long-running soap. They met and fell in love on the set over three decades ago. The Hayes have just written a book called *Like Sands through the Hourglass* about their lives on and off the set, and their affection for the fans.

"Some hold us so dearly in their hearts, the responsibility is touching and uplifting."

Susan says fans think they know the actors personally because they've invested so many years following the storylines.

"They're right too. The real personality tends to burn through any storyline after a while. You can't hide in a giant close-up."

Seaforth-Hayes met a concert pianist from Argentina recently who credits her with teaching him how to speak English in the late 1960s. When he wasn't attending music classes at Julliard in New York, he was watching Days of Our Lives.

On the flip side, a kidnapper and would-be killer was jailed in Pennsylvania after police found a hit list of his intended victims. It included the President of the United States, his entire cabinet, and Susan and her husband Bill.

Oh yeah, don't underestimate the passion of a dedicated soap fan.

When Global moved the Y and R to a new time slot a few years back, the switchboard lit up. Our long-suffering receptionist Rose remembers it well.

"We had senior citizens homes calling to complain because it really screwed up their suppertimes," Rose chuckles.

"The seniors wouldn't come to eat until the show was over."

But the soap's bubble may have burst.

Ratings for daytime dramas were at their peak in the 1980s with highly publicized romances like Luke and Laura's wedding on General Hospital.

Millions of fans were addicted, but the "trial of the century" forced them to go cold turkey. As O.J. Simpson struggled to put on the leather glove, soap fans were force-fed wall-to-wall coverage of the sensational murder trial.

In the beginning, the networks were swamped with complaints, but as the weeks went by, soap viewers found other ways to fill the void, and many simply never went back.

The numbers may be dwindling, but the fans that are left are fanatical.

"They just live, eat, breathe, and sleep it," says David Shark Fralick.

"And I guess they talk about it during lunch or on their smoke breaks. It's amazing that passion for a facade."

Actor Bill Hayes sums it up this way: "Soaps are enduring because they are stories, and everybody loves stories. They reflect real-life problems. The characters become part of the family, so that when we move to a different city they are still with us. And they give shut-in viewers a fantasy existence that can — for a while — lift them out of their own illnesses, difficulties and pains."

Long live the soaps. ■

7

Give Me Shelter

8

Global Edmonton lobby - Christmas 2006 - donations collected for Edmonton women's shelters

Give Me Shelter

The building has bulletproof glass, digital surveillance, high security fencing and alarm buttons. It's not a jail – it's a haven for women and children literally running for their lives.

They are desperate.

Janet arrived straight from the hospital with a five-day-old son, and a face so swollen, shelter staff couldn't tell what she was supposed to look like. Her partner had beaten her because the newborn wouldn't stop crying.

Karen was so terrified when she arrived at the shelter, she threw up in the office garbage can while recounting her story of abuse.

Edmonton police officers brought Diane to the shelter. Her partner had actually sold her to another man and her life was in serious danger.

You think you don't know these women, but you're wrong. Look a little closer.

She sits next to you at work – lives just down the block – she might be one of your friends, or relatives. Too many of us see the warning signs and don't act. We underestimate the danger, we feel uncomfortable asking if things are OK.

8

He might seem like a jerk to us, but if she's happy it's her life right? Wrong.

I worked with a sweet young woman once who's new boyfriend seemed like a real prize. He was handsome and attentive, and I was thrilled for her. But a few months into the relationship it became obvious this guy had real issues. He was insanely jealous and controlling, convinced she was having an affair. If we were having a girl's get-together, he would circle the block, calling repeatedly from a pay phone to make sure she wasn't "cheating" on him. We were concerned, but didn't know what to do, so we did nothing. I'm ashamed about that now.

Did you know that the number one cause of death of pregnant women is domestic homicide? It's sickening that some men are so insecure, they see an unborn baby as a threat.

And there's a dangerous cycle at work here too. Studies show that most of the women who enter women's shelters come from dysfunctional or abusive families themselves, and have not learned to properly take care of their own children. Unfortunately, violence often begets violence.

It's a social crisis that Senator Romeo Dallaire says, "is unacceptable in a society that has the resources."

And if any province has the resources to help, it's oil rich Alberta. Last year, Alberta shelters admitted more than 6900 women and 6000 children. That's amazing, and I salute the hard working, under paid and over worked shelter workers who literally saved the lives of these desperate families.

That's the good news. The bad news is - 20,000 women and children in crisis were turned away because there just wasn't room. That's unacceptable, and I was shocked to learn that in one of the wealthiest provinces in Canada, shelter capacity remains unfunded.

Consider this. Thunder Bay, Ontario, with a metro population of 122,000 people, has 48 shelter beds in Thunder Bay proper, and 30 more in the surrounding area. That's one bed for every 1500 people.

The Edmonton region has a population of approximately one million, with 114 funded shelter beds. That's one bed for every 8700 people.

We worry about building new bridges and filling potholes, but we don't seem as concerned about maintaining the social infrastructure.

The front line workers in the war on domestic violence say abuse in the home is a community issue that calls for a community response. The shelter staff cannot fight this battle alone.

So consider what you can do to help. Volunteer on the crisis line – donate cash or clothing to your local women's shelter - maybe lobby your MLA for more shelter funding.

That's what this book is all about. It was made possible by the generosity and good will of an Edmonton man named Richard McCallum. His company McCallum Printing is absorbing the full costs of printing this book, so 100 per cent of the proceeds can go to women's shelters in the Edmonton area. The money is desperately needed.

So thank you Richard, and thank you readers for buying this book.

It's one small step toward helping women and children live a life free of violence, and that is the greatest gift of all. ■

ABOUT THE AUTHOR

Lynda Steele anchors and co-produces Edmonton's only 5.00 PM newscast, the Early News on Global Edmonton, and teams up with Gord Steinke at 6.00 PM to co-anchor the News Hour. Together they are Edmonton's longest running anchor team.

Lynda was born in Edmonton, and grew up in Hinton. Although the award-winning broadcast journalist has spent a large part of her career in the City of Champions, Lynda has worked in local and national television newsrooms across western Canada.

Widely regarded as one of Alberta's most respected, trusted, and talented broadcast journalists, and voted Edmonton's most popular television news anchor three times, Lynda is proud to represent Global Edmonton at several community events each year, and has a special fondness for events that promote literacy, and raise awareness about domestic violence. Lynda has a passion for storytelling and the business of television news. Her work has been honoured with the Canadian Television Programming Association (CANPRO) Gold Award for best feature reporting in Canada, and the Alberta Motion Picture Industries Association (AMPIA), has named Lynda best journalist, best female news anchor, and best host for Lynda Steele Presents, a special series of half-hour interview shows.

In 2004, Lynda made a foray into the world of print journalism. You can read her lifestyles column Fridays in the Edmonton Journal.

photo courtesy Bruce Edwards